T0334692

Cambridge Elements ≡

Elements in New Religious Movements

Series Editor

Rebecca Moore

San Diego State University

Founding Editor

†James R. Lewis

Wuhan University

THE SACRED FORCE OF STAR WARS JEDI

William Sims Bainbridge

Independent Scholar

CAMBRIDGE
UNIVERSITY PRESS

CAMBRIDGE
UNIVERSITY PRESS

Shaftesbury Road, Cambridge CB2 8EA, United Kingdom

One Liberty Plaza, 20th Floor, New York, NY 10006, USA

477 Williamstown Road, Port Melbourne, VIC 3207, Australia

314–321, 3rd Floor, Plot 3, Splendor Forum, Jasola District Centre,
New Delhi – 110025, India

103 Penang Road, #05–06/07, Visioncrest Commercial, Singapore 238467

Cambridge University Press is part of Cambridge University Press & Assessment,
a department of the University of Cambridge.

We share the University's mission to contribute to society through the pursuit of
education, learning and research at the highest international levels of excellence.

www.cambridge.org
Information on this title: www.cambridge.org/9781009512213

DOI: 10.1017/9781009512206

First published 2024

A catalogue record for this publication is available from the British Library.

ISBN 978-1-009-51221-3 Hardback
ISBN 978-1-009-51216-9 Paperback
ISSN 2635-232X (online)
ISSN 2635-2311 (print)

The Sacred Force of Star Wars Jedi

Elements in New Religious Movements

DOI: 10.1017/9781009512206
First published online: December 2024

William Sims Bainbridge
Independent Scholar

Author for correspondence: William Sims Bainbridge, wsbainbridge@gmail.com

Abstract: As secularization threatens the stability of traditional religions, *Star Wars* provides a case study of how key functions of religion may transfer to innovative organizations and subcultures that challenge conventional definitions of faith, sacredness, and revival. This Element therefore examines the vast community of fans, especially gamers, who have turned *Star Wars* into a pararitual, providing them with a sense of the meaning of life and offering psychological compensators for human problems. The research methods include ethnography, participant observation, census of roles played by gaming participants, and recommender system statistics. The Element also shows the genetic connections between *Star Wars* and its predecessors in science fiction. Investigating the *Star Wars* fandom phenomenon – which involves hundreds of thousands of people – illustrates how audience cults and client cults evolve. Ultimately, *Star Wars* remains culturally and economically significant as we approach completion of its first half-century.

Keywords: Jedi, Star Wars, secularization, cult, pararituligion

ISBNs: 9781009512213 (HB), 9781009512169 (PB), 9781009512206 (OC)
ISSNs: 2635-232X (online), 2635-2311 (print)

Contents

Introduction to Star Wars

A long time ago in a galaxy far, far away, or in 1977 during the original *Star Wars* movie, Admiral Motti called the Jedi an "ancient religion," Han Solo called it a "hokey religion," and Governor Tarkin told Darth Vader: "The Jedi are extinct, their fire has gone out of the universe. You, my friend, are all that's left of their religion." Yet for nearly half a century, *Star Wars* has not merely imagined a fictional Jedi religion, but has also developed a new movement that may be well adapted for our real world today, and possesses various qualities of religion for a diversity of members. In *Journal of the American Academy of Religion*, Lyden (2012: 775) observed: "If there is any popular culture phenomenon that can be referred to as 'religion,' it would be the fandom associated with the *Star Wars* films." The most popular *Star Wars* video on YouTube, as of January 27, 2024, was a chant of the musical theme, that had earned 383,955,661 views and 34,089 written comments.[1]

Analyzing how the Internet has made possible many forms of digital religion, Campbell (2013: 57) observed: "Early online communities opened up new possibilities for social interaction, challenging traditional notions of community." The Jedi community is far more than fans of old movies and new streaming television programs; it now includes tens of thousands of authors who post literature online and hundreds of thousands of explorers in computer games that can function as virtual galaxies. Within this wide and diverse community, a small number of spiritual adventurers have even sought to become real Jedi knights, while larger numbers have incorporated aspects of the mythos in their personalities. As secularization has blurred the boundaries of faith, *Star Wars* has emerged as a leading *parareligion*, which is sometimes defined as a folk religion or a cultural movement that exists on the boundaries of established religions. It provides spiritual experiences, ethical guidance, and for the most devoted members a deep sense of the meaning of life, despite lack of faith in any god.

Star Wars began as a trilogy of popular movies, 1977–1983, that from the very beginning expanded to include novels, toys, games, and some television programs. The second trilogy of movies was not launched until 1999–2005, but was set a generation earlier in the history of the universe. The science fiction background was a galaxy with many habitable planets that could quickly be visited by flying spaceships through an imaginary *hyperspace*. The supernatural background was a mysterious Force that held the universe together and could be applied by rare individuals having unusual spiritual abilities or training. Hammer and Swartz-Hammer (2024: 9, 15) have documented how new religions often place ethical principles "within a cosmological framework," and "such narratives

---

[1] www.youtube.com/watch?v=ZTLAx3VDX7g.

may have features that situate them in an indeterminate space between the secular and the religious."

In the first film, a young lad named Luke Skywalker became the apprentice of Obi-Wan Kenobi, a hermit on the desert planet, Tatooine, who had been a Jedi Master before the Empire had seized power. He explained to Luke that "the Force is what gives the Jedi his power. It's an energy field created by all living things. It surrounds us and penetrates us. It binds the galaxy together." It "can have a strong influence on the weak-minded," and thus is "a powerful ally." A key paradox is that it both "controls your actions" and "obeys your commands." Obi-Wan mysteriously left this life willingly, but returned as a supernatural spirit in the 1980 second movie, *The Empire Strikes Back*, and told Luke to fly to the Dagobah planet for instruction by an even more senior Jedi Master, Yoda. There, Yoda taught Luke levitation and other magical powers, saying "my ally is The Force. And a powerful ally it is. All of life feeds it and makes it grow. Its energy surrounds us and binds us. Luminous beings are we, not this crude matter. Feel it you must. Feel the flow. Feel The Force around you." One might speculate that Luke Skywalker was the avatar of the creator of *Star Wars*, George Lucas, given the similarity of the names Luke and Lucas, who came to the planet Earth to teach us about the supernatural Force.

Central to the narratives of the first two trilogies was competition between two very different ways of relating to the Force: (1) Jedi who strictly avoided exploiting their powers for their own gain and who served the freedom and justice of the Republic government or its revival as Rebels, and (2) Sith who sought personal power and emotional satisfaction through the Force, often using it to promote the Empire or some other selfish dictatorship. In the context of the new World Wide Web, the second trilogy of movies encouraged a few *Star Wars* fans to begin creating small groups in hopes of establishing their own Jedi cultural movement, communicating largely online. In 1998, a general online archive for amateur fiction, named FanFiction.Net, allowed fans to publish freely their own stories set in the mythos, and in 2003 an online virtual world named *Star Wars Galaxies* allowed fans to pretend they lived together on its planets.

Commercial revival of the franchise stimulated extensive experimentation with various paths to Jediism, including attempts to obtain legal status for a Jedi Church, that sometimes failed and sometimes succeeded. Worldwide, there were many *Star Wars* fans who personally wished to get more directly involved in Force-related social and spiritual activities, but they were not geographically concentrated, so they could not easily establish local churches and their activities were primarily via Internet. That implies that many of the online participants may have been socially isolated in their home environments, for whatever reason, and sought subjective social status through online proclamation of the

Jedi culture that had belonged only to a very few social isolates like Obi-Wan, Luke and Yoda in the original *Star Wars* series.

On October 30, 2012, the Disney corporation purchased the Lucasfilm company that held the central copyrights and trademarks. A third trilogy of films was released 2015–2019 that depicted the near extinction of Jedi, and Disney distributed fully dozens of streaming episodes of five loosely connected series that gave precious little attention to the religious potential of Jediism, instead focusing on brutal violence around characters who had complex social relations with each other. Thus, the commercial background for Jediism has become problematic, but many of the numerous computer games allow players to assume the identity of Jedi Knights and experience adventures while possessing magical powers.

The first *Star Wars* video game I explored myself was *Super Star Wars* for the Super Nintendo, soon after it launched in 1992. It summarizes the first movie's story in a series of action scenes, typically where Luke Skywalker must kill many enemies, often jumping across gaps between places he can stand, what is called "platforming" in gamer lingo. About a third of the way through, Luke reaches Obi-Wan Kenobi's hermit home and the R2-D2 *droid* (robot with a personality) plays the crucial message from Princess Leia: "General Kenobi! Years ago you served my father in the Clone Wars. Now he begs you to help him in his struggle against the Empire. I have placed information vital to the survival of the rebellion into the memory system of this R2-unit. You must see this droid safely delivered to him on Yavin. This is our most desperate hour. Help me Obi-Wan Kenobi. You are our only help." While the game adds extensive combat on the planet Tatooine, it fails even to mention the original destination, Alderaan, jumping instead to Yavin, leaving out most of the interpersonal relations as well as the entire destruction of a planet. This example illustrates how complex the Jedi culture has become, often adjusting the material derived from the original movies, even while giving them a supportive new context.

1 Reconceptualizing Religion

George Lucas created a pair of religion-related films that can serve to frame his invention of the Jedi in the original 1977 *Star Wars* movie. His 1971 movie, *THX 1138*, is a complex allegory that seems anti-religious, set in a city that is like a prison based on technological oppression and brainwashing, in which personal freedom is totally suppressed. Cormier (1990: 195) explained why few people rebel: "their drug-soothed catatonic stupor is pacified by OMM, an unemotional God whose philosophy is repeated ad nauseam, 'work hard, increase production, prevent accidents, and be happy.'" A special wiki for the

Lucasfilm franchise summarizes the story that effectively explores this dystopia, including "an area reserved for the monks of OMM" and a computer that reveals "OMM does not, in fact, exist; his supposed responses in the Unichapels consist of a few simple pre-recorded phrases."[2]

Wikipedia's article about *THX 1138* includes an image of a famous painting and explains: "Hans Memling's Christ Giving His Blessing (1478) is used as the visual representation of the state-sanctioned deity OMM 0000."[3] Scholars may want to search multiple sources when factual accuracy is crucial, even conceptualizing Wikipedia as a search engine rather than encyclopedia, following links to read the regular publications an article cites. That article primarily cites a documentary disk published with the 2004 "director's cut" update of the movie and offers links to a dozen articles about members of the movie's cast. In 2007, someone using the name OMM0000 added a confession booth to YouTube, with this instruction: "Write your confessions in the comment box." From behind the face of Memling's Christ, an unemotional voice responded to a confession, repeating: "Yes, I understand." "Yes, fine." "Could you be more specific?" "You are a true believer." Despite gaining 27,895 views over the following 16 years, only 99 people chose to comment, and one was less than devoted: "This whole sequence creeps me out. I went looking for it because I saw this movie in my final year at high school and used to quote it word for word for my friends. It seamlessly blends capitalist doctrine with fundamentalist religion. Brilliant and scary. And that voice . . ."[4]

Released in 1981, between the second and third *Star Wars* movies, *Raiders of the Lost Ark* was based on ideas earlier developed by George Lucas. The protagonist, Indiana Jones, was a professor of archaeology who in 1936 competed with a French archaeologist named Belloq, who was in league with the Nazis, to find the lost Ark of the Covenant, which had supernatural powers and may have contained the original tablets on which the Ten Commandments were written. It is possible that these sacred objects really existed in ancient times, although we can doubt the Old Testament report in Joshua 3 that they magically opened the waters of the river Jordan so the Israelites could walk safely across. Jones and Belloq had their own reasons to go raiding for the Ark, but the Nazis could have used it in the coming war, for example marching their armies across the English Channel. In any case, the Ark is an artifact of great significance, that reveals one of the prime reasons why the general public may value archaeology: *The meaning of our lives today may be found in the distant past.* As Wikipedia reminds us, "Since its disappearance from the Biblical narrative, there have

---

[2] lucasfilm.fandom.com/wiki/THX_1138.   [3] en.wikipedia.org/wiki/THX_1138.
[4] www.youtube.com/watch?v=o_8YJGdyxxE.

been a number of claims of having discovered or of having possession of the Ark, and several possible places have been suggested for its location."[5]

Writing about *Raiders of the Lost Ark* in *The Biblical Archaeologist*, Hoberman (1983: 113) observed: "Few of the film's viewers were aware that an ancient Semitic legend also tells of a successful 'Ark-napping,' albeit without such sensational touches as Nazis, snakes, and submarines." The legend asserts that the Ark is currently held in a particular temple in Ethiopia, probably in Aksum. In *Journal of Religion in Africa*, Heldman (1992: 224) reported that Menelek was the son of Solomon and the Queen of Sheba: "When he returned home to Ethiopia, he took with him the Ark of the Covenant or *tābot* from Solomon's Temple." In *Journal of Black Studies*, Miriam Ma'at-Ka-Re Monges (2002: 235), whose middle name is a collage of ancient Egyptian religious terms, argued that from the Queen of Sheba we may learn "the importance of focusing on the logic of the intellect and on the wisdom of the larger, more holistic, intuitive inner self." Yet after Indiana Jones retrieves the Ark, it loses significance, is merely placed in a US government archive and apparently forgotten. The technical term in film criticism for losing interest in something that motivated much of a movie's action is spelled either MacGuffin or McGuffin (Lacy 2005), an infinitesimal detail that seems to imply that when professors finally complete their scholarship on a religious relic, their own work may also become trivial.

Clearly, George Lucas derived many components of his fantasies from real-world legends and religions, and many writers have concluded that Jediism is significantly derived from Zen Buddhism, Taoism, or other Asian spiritual traditions, which may or may not fully fit Western definitions of religion (Robinson 2005). The most obvious connection to Zen is the climax of the original movie, when Luke Skywalker and a team of allies are flying tiny spaceships in a mission to destroy the Death Star which has itself already destroyed Alderaan. It is vast and well armored, so Luke must find the exact moment to fire missiles through a narrow opening at a location that was not obvious. He hears the spiritual voice of Obi-Wan Kenobi, his deceased mentor: "Use the Force Luke. Let go!" Luke switches off his targeting equipment and follows his intuition, firing his missiles at exactly the correct moment.

This enacts the philosophy expressed in *Zen in the Art of Archery* by Eugen Herrigel (1953: 17; Shoji 2001) that postulates a spiritual *mindfulness* that guides an archer to shoot an arrow to the bullseye of the target, through "immediate experience of what, as the bottomless ground of Being, cannot be apprehended by intellectual means, and cannot be conceived or interpreted even after the most unequivocal and incontestable experiences: one knows it by not knowing it."

---

[5] en.wikipedia.org/wiki/Ark_of_the_Covenant.

In a book comparing how the *Star Wars* and *Star Trek* subcultures thrived in online virtual worlds, I had commented: "The Jedi seem very much like Zen masters, at least as they had been presented to Americans like George Lucas through popular literature" (Bainbridge 2016: 13). Herrigel was a disciple of D. T. Suzuki (1956), the most significant twentieth-century promoter of Zen outside Japan, and Alan Watts (1957) also built upon Suzuki's work. Both Suzuki and Watts saw similarities between Zen and psychotherapy, which suggests Zen was a secularized form of Buddhism, thus a parareligion (Suzuki, Fromm & De Martino 1960; Watts 1961). The westernized version of this Japanese tradition that emerged in the United States under Suzuki's influence is sometimes called "California Zen," because of its popularity there (Prohl 2014; Hori 2016; Chen 2022), and that was where George Lucas lived during Zen's surge from the 1950s. Especially relevant to his conception of the Jedi as warriors, as well as priests, is that Zen was often presented to Americans during that period as the religion of the Samurai and ideologically consistent with military violence (Sharf 1993).

The connection to Taoism is typically mentioned in relation to the Force. Wetmore (2000: 94) reported: "Unlike the Western notion of God, an authoritative, anthropomorphic patriarch, the Tao is both life giving and binding, yet does not actively control human beings or demand worship or authority." He argued that both Taoism and the Force of Jediism are based on a concept of the "flow" of energy, and he even suggested that the evil Empire represented European colonialism, while Asian Taoism could achieve liberation. Many other scholars had remarked upon the clear religious aspects of a mythological universe pervaded by the Force, even if it seemed to lack connections to Christianity (Decker & Eberl 2005; Christopher 2006; McDowell 2007; Possamai 2011).

Globalization and secularization in many post-industrial societies are blurring the traditional definition of "religious," especially with respect to new religious movements (Barker 2014) and those that are active online (Grieve 2013). The god-centric definition of religion was the historical result of the vast influence of the Jewish-Christian-Islamic monotheistic traditions that arose in one small corner of the world. Earlier polytheistic religions of Europe did not concentrate meanings in a single supernatural deity, for example not asserting that all existence had been created by Odin or Jupiter. Indeed, while we cannot here undertake the difficult analysis of ancient Indo-European religion, much of the surviving European folklore indicates that the gods were not fully supernatural, but dwelling within the world of Nature, while possessing greater powers than mere Humans possess. Thinking along those lines could imply that *secularization is in great measure repaganization*, returning to a time in which people are inspired by incoherent systems of myths, many of which may express personal hopes and ethical concerns through metaphoric narratives (Bainbridge 2015, 2023c).

The online Perseus archive of classic Greek and Roman culture defines "religio" from Latin into English as "conscientiousness, sense of right, moral obligation, duty," with no implication of supernaturalism.[6] Chidester (2003: 72) has observed: "Although its precise etymology remains uncertain, the Latin term, *religio*, whatever it meant, was inevitably defined in antiquity as the opposite of *superstitio*, which was understood as conduct based on ignorance, fear, and fraud." In a chapter titled "Secular Religion," Jacobsson and Lindblom (2016: 78) reported: "Many scholars have noted that secular belief systems can possess qualities and display features similar to religion without having a spiritual base or belief in a transcendent reality."

We need not settle here upon a new definition of "religion" in an apparently secular era, because *Star Wars* can best be understood in terms of multiple meanings that apply best to one or another subgroup or individual Jedi. The initial trilogy of movies, issued 1977–1983, described a time in the galactic past when indeed no organized Jedi religious organization still existed, and the only visible manifestations were two elderly Jedi Masters who had escaped into remote hermit homes, Obi-Wan Kenobi and Yoda. In sequence, but quickly dying, they mentored Luke Skywalker to become a Jedi, but this did not lead to any widespread revival of their ancient religion. Indeed, at this point Jediism (or Jedism) was a spiritual training that one master taught one student, implying that in our real world enthusiasts for the *Star Wars* culture could adopt it as their form of individual spirituality, without any church or temple. Social scientists have begun to debate whether individual spirituality should be defined as a sector of religion, versus being beyond the border of the sacred (Oh & Sarkisian 2012; Ammerman 2013; Miller 2016). However, some later components of the now vast *Star Wars* mythos were set thousands of years earlier in galactic history, when Jediism was an influential religion, although represented by an elite monastic order within a society in which only very unusual people possessed supernatural powers. While the subsequent individualism of the Jedi may seem to weaken any definition as a religion, in a secular society that may in fact be a major mode of religious revival.

Scholars have proposed many different terms to describe social and cultural phenomena that resemble "religion" without quite meeting all the criteria of its popular definition. Two decades ago, I began using the term *parareligion* to describe the New Age movement (Bainbridge 2004: 382). Parareligions of many different kinds cover the broad territory around established religions, and

---

[6] www.perseus.tufts.edu/hopper/morph?l=Religio&la=la.

thus may be defined as attenuated forms of faith, liberated components of established denominations, or distinct subcultures that perform functions similar to one or more of those that traditionally belonged to sacred institutions. Demerath (2000: 2) had already defined *parareligion* as comparable to "invisible religion, folk religion, implicit religion and quasi-religion."

For a study of computer games based on Korean folk religions, I suggested a subcategory of parareligion: "In the context of modern secularization, *legendism* can be defined as a cultural form adjacent to traditional religion, taking supernatural narratives seriously but not devoting faith or authority to them" (Bainbridge 2023b: 55). The term *invented religion* has been proposed by Cusack (2010: 4), not merely to describe several recent examples of parody religions, but significantly a few cases like Jediism that advocates judged "was a fiction so good it should actually be true." In the World Religions and Spirituality Project, Davidsen (2018) praised the real-world Jediism derived from the imaginary Jedi Knights: "The Jedi Community is a fiction-based religious milieu." Definitely, the term "fiction-based" is accurate in this context, but it may suggest something about the complex media of communication in our current age, when fiction may serve as a bridge between cultures of many different kinds.

In the early 1960s, anthropologist Colin Turnbull and I often discussed his extensive research in Africa, including his pioneer recordings of the music of the Pygmies, and I learned that the oldest and most sacred song of one community, which they thought of as their own heritage, was in fact the American song, "Oh My Darling, Clementine" (cf. Grinker 2000: 95), that an ancestor must have learned from a traveler. This prepared me to ponder the extent to which all religions that arose in early preliterate societies may have incorporated tales that were originally invented as fiction, and retold expansively from generation to generation. This is the mirror image of *euhemerism*, the ancient Greek theory of Euhemerus that the gods are merely exaggerated tales about real people of the historical past (Bainbridge 2013: 13; Hobson 2017). Also, to the extent that George Lucas drew upon Zen and Taoism when inventing Jediism, it inherited some of their religious authenticism. In *Dynamic Secularization*, I acknowledged that Jediism does not seem to have a god:

> Its fundamental principle, the Force, lacks consciousness, but is an energy field that permits Jedi to perceive, communicate, and even perform actions psychically. In the original 1977 movie, Obi-Wan Kenobi is able to influence the thoughts of enemy storm troopers, and appears to provide guidance to Luke Skywalker even after death. In the 1980 sequel, the magical powers of the Jedi become more visible and thus open to possible disproof, as Luke, Yoda and Darth Vader are able to move physical objects by power of the mind

alone. The second trilogy of movies provides an obscure interpretation of the Force that explains it in pseudoscientific rather than religious terms, referring to Force-generating "midi-chlorians" that exist inside living cells and may be more numerous in the cells of Jedi. Thus, one of the challenges for real-world Jedi groups is how seriously they will take the supernatural or pseudoscientific aspects. (Bainbridge 2017: 123)

The *Star Wars* mythos and subculture of devoted enthusiasts are so complex, that here we must efficiently mention many representative examples, and also use quantitative data when available to map vast territories that border on the supernatural. For example, checking Wikipedia for Obi-Wan Kenobi reveals that his page was viewed 1,544,178 times in the year 2022, while Yoda's page was viewed only 451,808 times.[7] Does that mean that Yoda was only 29.3 percent as religiously significant? Not exactly. Looking closely at the data reveals that Obi-Wan Kenobi got a huge jump in pageviews, 55,463 on May 27, 2022, and many around that day, which Yoda did not get. Further searching revealed what would have been obvious to a member of the Jedi subculture. A new TV series with the exact name *Obi-Wan Kenobi* launched on May 27, 2022, getting 383,656 Wikipedia pageviews that day on its own new page, and 6,816,413 that year, stimulating interest in the older article with similar title and topic.[8]

One obvious conclusion is that the commercial industry, constantly producing new products of many kinds, has great influence over the folk subculture, and only small fractions of the enthusiasts who personally adopt the values and concepts of the Jedi will belong to formally independent Jedi organizations. The wider context of secularization may possibly be to the advantage of new forms of religion, especially if they do not fit traditional definitions of "church" or "theology." For example, a recent comprehensive study of secularization identifies one of its main factors as *differentiation*: "the separation of religion from various aspects of societies, institutions, or individuals" (Kasselstrand, Zuckerman & Cragun 2023: 25). Thus, the separation of church and state may weaken the church, but an innovative cult may gain strength by connecting not with the government but with commercial business. Also, the combination of secularization with globalization may erode the traditional western definition of religion in terms of faithful Bible-based monotheism, opening more room for godless magic, and shifting academic analysis to the dynamics of the human mind that support supernatural hopes.

In the previous century, Rodney Stark and I developed a formal theory of religion based on established traditions of sociology and cognitive psychology (Stark & Bainbridge 1985, 1987). Starting with the behavioral principle that

---

[7] en.wikipedia.org/wiki/Obi-Wan_Kenobi; en.wikipedia.org/wiki/Yoda.
[8] en.wikipedia.org/wiki/Obi-Wan_Kenobi_(TV_series).

humans seek rewards and avoid costs whenever feasible, we suggested that psychological *compensators* are postulations of reward according to explanations that are not readily susceptible to unambiguous evaluation. Many highly valuable rewards are difficult or even impossible to obtain, most obviously immortality but also high social status and stability in a chaotic world. We then defined *religion* as a system of psychological *general compensators* based on supernatural assumptions, and *magic* as unverified means to obtain more specific rewards such as cure of a physical disability or mild neurosis.

The meaning of the term *supernatural* depends of course on what phenomena we consider to be natural, and that has become a very painful challenge in our current era of widespread secularization. To an Atheist, a supernatural being is one that does not exist but is believed in by some ignorant people. To a more Humane philosopher, supernatural beings include all deceased people, who hopefully continue to exist in some afterlife, even though they were never gods. Julius Caesar wrote about how such supernatural beliefs strengthened his enemies, the Gauls: "They wish to inculcate this as one of their leading tenets, that souls do not become extinct, but pass after death from one body to another, and they think that men by this tenet are in a great degree excited to valor, the fear of death being disregarded."[9]

We may remember the Twilight of the Gods that took place during the first performance of Richard Wagner's opera *Götterdämmerung* in 1876. Near the end, hero Siegfried has died and his beloved Brünnhilde prepares to join him in death within his funeral pyre: "a bright fire fastens on my heart to embrace him, enfolded in his arms, to be one with him in the intensity of love!"[10] Yet she is neither an ordinary woman nor a deity, but a Valkyrie who has often ridden between natural and supernatural realms. Indeed, she whispers to us that there is no clear distinction between natural and supernatural within many Indo-European or Pagan religions. Yet from the standpoint of modern science, we have already noted that both the Force wielded by Jedi, and the Hyperspace through which all interstellar spaceships fly, are supernatural concepts unrelated to superstitions about deities.

Stark and I often used the word *cult* not with the negative connotations many people apply, but respectfully as an unconventional subculture akin to religion, and I even suggested "cult is culture writ small" (Bainbridge 1978: 14). Considering the spectrum of compensators from general to specific, we proposed three compatible models of cult formation, one of which was the *entrepreneur model*, in which an individual or a small company launches a new business using at least some general

---

[9] Julius Caesar, *Gallic War*, www.perseus.tufts.edu/hopper/text?doc=Perseus%3Atext% 3A1999.02.0001%3Abook%3D6%3Achapter%3D14.

[10] www.rwagner.net/libretti/gotterd/e-gott-a3s3.html.

compensators based on supernatural or undefined assumptions (Bainbridge & Stark 1979). Indeed, definition of religions as nonprofit organizations may support their claim to sacred rights not enjoyed by merchants, and the development of the legal concept of "nonprofit" was influenced in recent centuries by established religions (DiMaggio & Anheier 1990). However, independent religious entrepreneurs may personally profit from their sacred work (Bainbridge 2002). Unless we share the faith of a particular organization, we may have no valid philosophical reason for judging it to be holy.

One of the most active independent organizations considered in this Element is The Temple of the Jedi Order which reportedly registered in Texas in 2005. However, it appears that the government of that state allows nonprofit organizations to submit forms and does not go through any evaluation process until the organization also requests exemption from taxation by the federal government, and it does not at all distinguish religious from nonreligious organizations.[11] The Temple's website says: "Temple of the Jedi Order (TotJO) is a legally recognized Jedi Church and ministry of Jediism."[12] But the supportive document it links to says nothing about religion, while approving tax exempt status for it as a nonprofit charity.[13]

On December 16, 2016, the Charity Commission for England and Wales had rejected the application of The Temple of the Jedi Order to register as a religion, complaining: "The Commission is not satisfied that TOTJO is established for exclusively charitable purposes for the advancement of religion and/or the promotion of moral and ethical improvement for the benefit of the public."[14] Nations differ greatly in how they formally recognize the religious status of an organization, partly depending upon the degree of their separation of church and state, but also in the confusion of rapid secularization in large segments of the world. In the context of England and Wales, Holmes (2017) thoughtfully observed that the traditional legal definition of a religious charity as theistic was abandoned because "When the Charities Act 2006 was passing through the House of Commons, some MPs observed that this was unsatisfactory, since a number of religions are non-theistic." But no new legal definition of religion was adopted.

Whatever its origins, if a small cult evolved in the direction of being a full religion, Stark and I called it a *cult movement*. If it offered magical services, we called it a *client cult*, existing in the conceptual territory between a religion and a business. But many cases fit a third category, such as occult magazines or *Star*

---

[11] www.sos.state.tx.us/corp/nonprofitfaqs.shtml.

[12] www.templeofthejediorder.org/index.php/faq.

[13] www.templeofthejediorder.org/images/TOTJO-IRS-Exemption-Letter.pdf.

[14] assets.publishing.service.gov.uk/media/5a7f1b5c40f0b62305b851d9/Temple_of_the_Jedi_Order_FINAL_DECISION.pdf.

Wars movies, which we called an *audience cult* (Bainbridge & Stark 1980) in which followers were passive and their costs were low. To the extent that fans of *Star Wars* became disciples, and they grew very active in promoting and expanding the subculture, then their *audience cult* would have evolved into a *cult movement* and fully earned the adjective *religious*.

Many sources report that George Lucas became very interested in Joseph Campbell's analysis of the world's mythologies about heroes, but it is not clear how much it influenced the main *Star Wars* narrative. Here, we can use it to introduce a somewhat different analysis of the religious quality experienced by the audience. Campbell's perspective was largely built upon van Gennep's 1909 book, *The Rites of Passage*, which Campbell (2005: 23) summarized thus:

> The standard path of the mythological adventure of the hero is a magnification of the formula represented in the rites of passage: *separation – initiation – return*: which might be named the nuclear myth of the monomyth. A hero ventures forth from the world of common day into a region of supernatural wonder (x): fabulous forces are there encountered and a decisive victory is won (y): the hero comes back from this mysterious adventure with the power to bestow boons on his fellow man (x).

While this model fits some of the stories in *Star Wars*, I suggest it even better fits the experience of the fans and disciples, who temporarily leave our mundane world to experience a different galaxy, then return home after the movie is over. In computer games, they are even able to perform actions and make decisions for many hours, from within an identity and environment different from their ordinary lives. The new identity in games is an *avatar*, a term derived from spirit possession in Hindu religion. Snodgrass (2023: xiii) has examined in depth how "avatars can provide the possessed and gamer alike with perceived superior second identities and social standings." Religions from different regions of the world differ in the emphasis they give to prayer versus meditation, which are personal religious experiences, but only prayer engages God. I suggest there is a third personal religious ritual, vicarious experience of a spiritually superior identity, comparable to spirit possession but voluntary, what Snodgrass calls *ecstatic transformations*. While today we tend to define *ecstasy* as overpowering happiness, in ancient Greece that connotation was based on the primary meaning of departing from one's normal self-identity.[15] Snodgrass uses the term to connect spirit possession with playing the role of an avatar in a computer game.

Today we can suggest that parareligions are diverse socio-cultural phenomena that exist at the conceptual boundary of organizations traditionally defined as religions. They may or may not explicitly use concepts like "god" or

---

[15] www.merriam-webster.com/dictionary/ecstatic.

"supernatural," but offer some form of general psychological compensator for the limitations of real life. Both the commercial and volunteer aspects of *Star Wars* culture may qualify as parareligions, but some of the noncommercial aspects seem much closer to being fully religious. The *Star Wars* culture or community is an excellent example for exploring modern parareligions, not only because it is somewhat familiar to almost everyone, but because it is complex, consisting of many components that have different relationships with religion. A general principle that may apply to many parareligions is that highly popular components involving deep personal investment of time and energy, such as the popular computer games, serve a diverse public, only some of whom may treat the Jedi like a religion. A related factor illustrated by the *Star Wars* culture is the contradictory impact of commercialization, in this case very successful promotion of the mythos by the Disney corporation that acquired ownership of it, which however seems to reduce its potentially sacred characteristics. Nearly half a century after its genesis, the Jedi continue to explore the uncertain territory between faith, hope, and despair.

2 Older Testaments

Before we consider how real-world mindfulness, spirituality and religion have emerged from the *Star Wars* mythos, we need to be aware of its cultural background. The original protagonist, Luke Skywalker, grew up on a desert planet named Tatooine that was comparable to Mars and two similar imaginary worlds, Barsoom and Arrakis. Unlike our actual "red planet," fictional planets often had well-established religious cultures. When George Lucas created *Star Wars*, he was significantly inspired by the "space opera" subculture within science fiction, which included serious authors like Edgar Rice Burroughs (1875–1950) who invented Barsoom and Frank Herbert (1920–1986) who invented Arrakis, but also upon the movie serial trio, *Flash Gordon* (1936–1940) that included Mars. Space opera may be defined as the science fiction "equivalent of horse opera (cowboy tales) and soap opera (domestic melodramas), consists of fantastic adventures set against a fanciful interplanetary background" (Bainbridge 1986: 77). A comparison with grand opera should be added, especially *Der Ring des Nibelungen* by Richard Wagner, applying Wagner's (1895) concept in a secular context to suggest that every religion is a *total work of art*.

Fans of these works of fiction are members of *audience cults*, that provide some of the psychological compensation for life's pains and problems that full religions do, but not requiring full faith or very significant investment of time and money. The religious implications and cultic quality of the best space opera are well illustrated by *A Princess of Mars* by Burroughs. Near the beginning of the twentieth century, astronomer Percival Lowell (1906, 1908) published popular books, titled *Mars and Its Canals* and *Mars as the Abode of Life*, claiming it was possible to live in the Martian environment, where a civilization may have built canals to distribute the diminishing supply of water. Burroughs built upon those ideas and framed the climax of his first novel around the failure of the atmosphere factories built by the high-tech Martians to stay alive as their low-gravity planet slowly lost its air. By the middle of the century, astronomers knew the Martian atmosphere was far too weak for humans to breathe, and we now know it is indeed primarily carbon dioxide (De Vaucouleurs 1950; Horowitz 1986).

John Carter did not fly to Mars in a rocket ship, but rather his spirit teleported there at the point of death on Earth in 1866, when he was prospecting for gold after having served as an officer in the defeated Confederate army during the Civil War. His reincarnation on Barsoom, and marriage to Princess Dejah Thoris, had qualities of moral salvation, because they belonged to different species, and thus transcended his Confederate racism. But another quality is shared by the original *Star Wars* story, namely how a socially isolated individual can gain social status through heroism. *A Princess of Mars* is written in the first person, and begins with remarkable phenomenology: "I do not know why I should fear death, I who have died twice and am still alive; but yet I have the same horror of it as you who have never died, and it is because of this terror of death, I believe, that I am so convinced of my mortality" (Burroughs 1917: 1).

The second novel in the long series, *Gods of Mars*, implies what many readers infer about Burroughs, that he was a critical opponent of religion as it existed on Earth. This time, John Carter was resurrected in the area near the south pole of the planet, that the dominant religion defined as Heaven, and where many Barsoomians voyaged to experience a glorious death. He soon met his old alien friend Tars Tarkas and a girl named Thuvia who would be a central character in the fourth book of the series. She was a prisoner in the Temple of Issus, ruled by the cannibalistic Holy Therns, who pretend to be the benign clergy for everyone, yet eat the flesh of the deceived believers who arrive on mistaken quests. Beset now by doubts about her people's traditional faith, Thuvia asked Carter if they should try to escape. He replied with what some readers might judge was merely an exaggerated criticism of conventional Earthly religion, and that *Star Wars* might borrow for the beginning of some future movie about escape from the evil Sith:

> We have the right to escape if we can ... Our own moral senses will not be offended if we succeed, for we know that the fabled life of love and peace in the blessed Valley of Dor is a rank and wicked deception. We know that the valley is not sacred; we know that the Holy Therns are not holy; that they are a race of cruel and heartless mortals, knowing no more of the real life to come than we do. Not only is it our right to bend every effort to escape – it is

a solemn duty from which we should not shrink even though we know that we should be reviled and tortured by our own peoples when we returned to them. Only thus may we carry the truth to those without, and though the likelihood of our narrative being given credence is, I grant you, remote, so wedded are mortals to their stupid infatuation for impossible superstitions, we should be craven cowards indeed were we to shirk the plain duty which confronts us. (Burroughs 1918: 66)

Advocates of secularization at this point might raise the issue that *Star Wars*, like much other science fiction including *THX 1138*, offers at best a parody of religion, or even a critique of it. Possession of supernatural powers can be corruptive, if they are allowed to serve personal desires rather than ethical principles. Yet many people today sense they lack divine guidance, and may be open to new forms of transcendence communicated via fantasies. Frank Herbert published the first of his very comparable novels about Arrakis, *Dune*, in 1965, drawing upon an already well-developed tradition that might be called *ethnography of imagined worlds*, of which Barsoom was the archetype. In 2021, Thomas Lethbridge explained a dozen memes he believed *Star Wars* inherited from *Dune*, including the desert planet Tatooine, and a black market drug available from spice mines. Notably, he speculated that the Jedi Order was derived from *Dune's* "Bene Gesserit cult – a matriarchal group manipulating events behind the scenes and often accused of witchcraft. Much like the Jedi, Bene Gesserit members can be found throughout the galaxy, highlighting their importance to the world of *Dune*."

In 2023, Ryan Britt argued that the female *Star Wars* cult called Nightsisters on the planet Dathomir was more directly derived from the Bene Gesserit, but now: "The Bene Gesserit are using the Force." In the sixth episode of the 2023 streaming video series *Star Wars: Ahsoka*, an enemy of the Jedi named Thrawn commented: "After all, death and resurrection are common deceptions played out by both Nightsister and Jedi." Ironically, the Nightsisters had been annihilated in the nineteenth episode of the fourth season of *The Clone Wars* animated series back in 2012, and were not resurrected. But the vast universe around Tatooine is constantly being visited during different years of its history, thus transporting the devoted fans through time as well as space.

In *The Making of Star Wars*, J. W. Rinzer says George Lucas acknowledged that his story belonged to "the grand tradition of Edgar Rice Burroughs's John Carter of Mars, and Alex Raymond's Flash Gordon." (Rinzer 2007: 47). In both of these popular mass media franchises, alien religions often seem selfishly evil, as the Therns resemble the Sith who follow the Dark Side of the Force. The King Features Syndicate noticed that the early science fiction comic strip, *Buck Rogers*, had become very popular after its launch in 1929, and began negotiations to develop a competing comic strip based on the Mars novels by Burroughs. When that effort failed, King Features created *Flash Gordon* with some of the features of both existing franchises.

From about 1913 to 1956, many local movie theaters offered special weekend events that were designed for families including children, that combined a feature film with one 20-minute episode of a serial, plus perhaps a cartoon or two. The first *Star Wars* film was subsequently renamed *Star Wars: Episode IV – A New Hope*, following the serial format, implying that it was the fourth episode with its own subtitle. In an interview, George Lucas said of *Flash Gordon*, "I just loved it when it was a movie serial on television; the original Universal serial was on television at 6:15 PM every day, and I was just crazy about it" (Rinzer 2007: 93). Today, many of them are freely available on YouTube and elsewhere. In all three *Flash Gordon* serials, the emperor of the planet Mongo, Ming the Merciless, attacks Earth from a distance. Ming must be thrice defeated by Flash in collaboration with his girlfriend, Dale Arden, and scientist Dr. Zarkov who has a rocket ship that flies them twice to Mongo and once to Mars.

As a devoted fan of *Flash Gordon*, George Lucas would have been deeply influenced by the first serial, which weaves exotic religion with romance, as *Star Wars* often does. Mongo worships the Great God Tao, pronounced TAY-oh and not connected to terrestrial Taoism. A *Flash Gordon* wiki reports: "Tao's temple is a holy site, off limits to visitors. It is accessible only through the Tunnel of Terror, which is guarded by the sacred Fire dragon."[16] Ming becomes attracted to Dale and forces her to undergo marriage to him, enacted by a high priest before a statue of Tao that had earlier represented the ancient Egyptian god Osiris in the 1932 horror movie, *The Mummy*, starring Boris Karloff.[17] Flash is able to disrupt the wedding, and Tao drops into the background for several episodes, apparently because Ming is angry at the high priest who failed to complete the ritual. A book about the *Flash Gordon* serials reveals that the actor playing the high priest was replaced with one "whose flamboyant theatricality was more appropriate to the role" (Kinnard, Crnkovich & Vitrone 2005: 44), secretly saving Ming from being killed by fire in Tao's Temple at the serial's climax.

Flash Gordon's Trip to Mars emphasizes magic and religion, especially through the character of Queen Azura who resembles a Jedi Master undecided between the Light and Dark sides of the Force. The Internet Movie Database explains that Ming the Merciless "has a new weapon: a deadly ray that crosses space to wreak havoc on earth. Earth's only hope is for our heroes to take off again and stop the ray at its source on Mars, where they (and a stowaway) must battle Ming's ally, Queen Azura, who turns her enemies into lumpish clay

---

[16] flashgordon.fandom.com/wiki/Great_God_Tao.
[17] burgcastlestein.blogspot.com/2013/06/osiris-tao-and-god-of-emerald-fingers.html.

people."[18] Note the functional equivalence of Ming's ray gun and the Death Star in the first *Star Wars* movie used by the evil Empire to destroy entire planets. The article about Queen Azura in the *Flash Gordon* wiki notes some ambiguity whether her magic is supernatural or based on secret science: "She displays several magical abilities, chiefly the power to teleport herself and others but also a degree of telekinesis and the power to transform individuals into Clay People, which may or may not be an acceleration of a process which can occur naturally within the Valley of Desolation."[19]

The third serial, *Flash Gordon Conquers the Universe*, had very direct connections to the first *Star Wars* movie, but lacked magic and religion. Each episode after the first begins with flashback text scrolling up and away to prepare those in the audience who had not seen the previous episode, like this introduction to the second episode that reminds us the real Second World War had actually begun by 1940: "Following the wake of dictators, war and rumors of war – a ravaging plague, the 'Purple Death,' strikes the earth. Flash Gordon and professor Zarkov, believing Ming The Merciless is behind the 'Purple Death,' start with Dale Arden in Zarkov's rocket ship for Mongo." Here is the equivalent scroll-up text from the first *Star Wars* movie: "It is a period of civil war. Rebel spaceships, striking from a hidden base, have won their first victory against the evil Galactic Empire."

At the climax of the last serial, Ming has filled one spaceship with "solarite" to destroy cities on Earth, but Flash captures it and flies toward the castle tower where Ming has barricaded himself. At the last moment, Flash parachutes to safety and Ming is killed. In parallel fashion, the climax of the first *Star Wars* movie requires Luke Skywalker to pilot a spaceship along exactly the right path immediately above the Death Star, and release missiles at the precise moment that only the magic of the Force could reveal. To be sure, George Lucas was inspired by other movies, and a YouTube channel named The Starkiller posted a video comparing attacks by British aircraft on German infrastructure in the 1955 film *The Dam Busters* with almost identical moments of the attack on the Death Star.[20]

George Lucas was also inspired by Akira Kurosawa's movies, made in Japan with some cultural content from Zen or Buddhism more generally. Movie journalist, Young (2019), who specializes in *Star Wars*, has observed: "When people talk about the cinematic influences of *Star Wars,* the first movie that will come out of most mouths will be *Flash Gordon*. The second, though, is almost always Akira Kurosawa's 1958 classic *The Hidden Fortress*. This film tells the tale of Japanese peasants trying to escape a war between provinces and find

---

[18] www.imdb.com/title/tt0030138/. [19] flashgordon.fandom.com/wiki/Queen_Azura.
[20] www.youtube.com/watch?v=lNdb03Hw18M.

themselves aiding a general and a princess on the run." In a video interview titled "George Lucas on Akira Kurosawa" on YouTube, George Lucas mentions *The Hidden Fortress* but says he was most impressed by Kurosawa's 1954 film, *Seven Samurai.*[21]

Several authors have explored the cultural connections to Buddhism (Bortolin 2015; Ross 2021), including even unconfirmed claims that George Lucas was personally inspired by a particular Tibetan colleague of the Dalai Lama (Littlefair 2015). When interviewed, Lucas was very cautious, and we may imagine he wanted to avoid losing many fans who might be hostile toward faiths other than their own. Especially detailed was a long interview with Bill Moyers that included many question-answer complexities like this one: "MOYERS: What do you make of the fact that so many people have interpreted your work as being profoundly religious?" "LUCAS: I don't see Star Wars as profoundly religious. I see Star Wars as taking all the issues that religion represents and trying to distill them down into a more modern and easily accessible construct – that there is a greater mystery out there" (Moyers & Lucas 1999).

Clearly, the *Star Wars* mythos borrowed from many sources, and we do not have adequate data to measure their varying significance. However, we can conclude this section with an overview of the early mythos itself, based primarily on data derived from the Netflix movie recommender system that was made public back in 2006 (Feuerverger, He & Khatri 2012). As Table 1 reports, the original 1977 film had been rated by 85,184 customers on a scale from 1 to 5, giving it a very high 4.50 mean score. *The Ewok Adventure* was a television special, while *Clone Wars: Vol. 1* was an animated television series.

The first three movies have very high Netflix mean scores, and the first has extremely strong correlations with ratings of the other two, 0.75 and 0.67 when 1.00 is the mathematical maximum. A methodological caution is that people who rated two movies needed to have seen both, which implies some of them were already fans of the mythos, which might distort the estimated correlation, especially when one film got fewer ratings than the other. *The Phantom Menace* and *Attack of the Clones* have much lower mean scores and correlations with the original *Star Wars*. The *Clone Wars* animated series has higher ratings which indeed justified another more extensive and graphically superior series on the same story beginning in 2008. But it had lower numbers of raters, implying that the people who viewed it are fans of animation, and the correlation is not high. The sixth movie, *Revenge of the Sith*, opened in theaters in 2005, but was apparently not yet available through Netflix, so the dataset does not have numbers for it.

---

[21] "George Lucas on Akira Kurosawa," www.youtube.com/watch?v=E9V2T1ONA2I.

Table 1 Popularity data of first five movies and comparisons

		2006 Netflix Data			
Title	**Year**	**Ratings**	**Score**	**IV: A New Hope**	
IV: A New Hope	1977	85,184	4.50	**Shared**	**Correl.**
V: Empire Strikes Back	1980	92,470	4.54	72,929	0.75
VI: Return of the Jedi	1983	88,846	4.46	69,423	0.67
The Ewok Adventure	1985	1,521	3.29	1,187	0.21
I: The Phantom Menace	1999	71,143	3.60	42,643	0.32
II: Attack of the Clones	2002	92,671	3.55	50,749	0.32
Clone Wars: Vol. 1	2004	21,603	4.10	17,157	0.30
Flash Gordon	1936	613	3.10	358	0.19
... Trip to Mars	1938	470	3.17	289	0.24
... Conquers the Universe	1940	427	3.13	267	0.21
Dune	1984	17,869	3.49	11,009	0.16
Frank Herbert's Dune TV	2000	6,320	3.63	3,981	0.17
Children of Dune TV	2003	4,925	3.69	3,121	0.19
Seven Samurai	1954	31,692	4.20	13,921	0.13
Hidden Fortress	1958	5,423	3.95	2,789	0.15
THX 1138	1971	8,265	3.08	4,873	0.07
Raiders of the Lost Ark	1981	118,212	4.50	63,485	0.30

Despite their lower ratings, the prequel films significantly encouraged fans to develop the Jediism subculture, for two reasons. First, the new World Wide Web that developed over the 1990s allowed them to communicate with like-minded fellows and develop enduring online social networks. Starting in 2003 they could even found durable online groups called *guilds* in the *Star Wars Galaxies* virtual world, and in 2004 the first of many Jedi groups launched in the non-game virtual world, *Second Life*.[22] Second, the movies depicted a time in the history of the galaxy when the Jedi were a respected religious organization serving significant functions for a civilization, rather than just a few hermit survivors of its downfall, as in the original series.

In *The Phantom Menace*, Yoda says to Anakin Skywalker: "Fear is the path to the dark side. Fear leads to anger. Anger leads to hate. Hate leads to suffering. I sense much fear in you." Searching Wikipedia for "Anakin Skywalker" opens the page for Darth Vader, which got 1,526,845 pageviews in 2022, because Anakin's identity changed after he was attracted to the dark side of the Force: "Originally a slave on Tatooine, Anakin Skywalker is a Jedi prophesied to bring

---

[22] swrp.fandom.com/wiki/Category:Jedi_organizations.

balance to the Force. He is lured to the dark side of the Force by Chancellor Palpatine and becomes a Sith Lord, assuming the name of Darth Vader and helping his new master all but destroy the Jedi Order."[23] Yoda's statement expresses the concern that leads the Jedi Council to refuse to accept Anakin as a student. The first actor who played Anakin was nine years old, but Jedi were supposed to begin training much younger to avoid already feeling fear and other disruptive emotions. Anakin's mother remained a slave back on Tatooine, after he was taken across the galaxy, so he already felt both fear and anger. Jedi Master Qui-Gon Jinn had essentially adopted Anakin and defied the Jedi Council by training him to be an independent Jedi. After Qui-Gon's death, Jedi Master Obi-Wan Kenobi took over that dubious task.

In the second film of the prequel trilogy, *Attack of the Clones*, complex mysteries reveal that war is coming, and the clones are thousands of duplicates of one powerful warrior, thus men robbed of individuality. In the first regular episode of *The Clone Wars* 2008 animated series, "Ambush," Yoda is on an adventure with a team of three clones and seeks to restore their right to individual identity, then proclaims: "Clones you may be. But the Force resides in all life-forms. Use it you can to quiet your mind." In *Attack of the Clones*, Anakin gained too much individuality when he reached young adulthood, falling in love with Padmé Amidala despite the celibacy required of Jedi. He then rushed too late to Tatooine to save his mother, slaughtering wildly everyone around her after she died in his arms. The prequel trilogy concluded in 2005 with *Revenge of the Sith*, as Anakin becomes Darth Vader, while Padmé Amidala dies in the birth of their twin children, Luke Skywalker and Leia Organa, central characters of the original trilogy. Thus, the prequel ended somewhat pessimistically about the value of the Force, even as it stimulated public interest again in *Star Wars*, apparently promoting a real-world Jedi community.

Near the bottom of Table 1, we see a very low correlation between ratings of the original 1977 *Star Wars* movie and its 1971 predecessor, *THX 1138*. One superficial critique might argue that George Lucas expressed general hostility to religion in 1971, but fans did not notice that bias in 1977. Another simplistic analysis might say that his theology favored Buddhism over Christianity, yet the relatively strong correlation with *Raiders of the Lost Ark* would seem to contradict that theory, given its biblical focus. While Lucas himself mentally combined the cultural memes he borrowed from several sources, most fans valued the drama of the movies, their special effects, and the meaningful relations between major characters. But in varying degrees, fans may also have sought new meaning in their own lives, a few ready to adopt a new

---

[23]　en.wikipedia.org/wiki/Darth_Vader.

religion, and many more interested in experiencing the parareligion offered in online social media and electronic games.

3 Online Social Groups

Long after *Return of the Jedi* in 1983, the subculture survived on memories and frequent release of related products, until the fourth film, *The Phantom Menace*, achieved a major revival in 1999. Set a generation before the original 1977 film, it described a time when the Jedi were well-organized, having even a central Jedi Council. It served essentially as a branch of government for the multi-planet Republic, focusing its energies on special reconnaissance and military missions, rather than serving local populations from community-based churches. Starting at least as early as December 1995, individual *Star Wars* fans had begun claiming the status of Jedi leader and sharing their ideas online.[24] Online research presents many unconventional ethical issues, such as ambiguities surrounding privacy when people post personal views online using pseudonyms or within closed social groups that later open up (Eynon, Fry & Schroeder 2008; Elm 2009; Johns 2013), so caution is required. Some Jedi activists formed online groups, many of which seemed temporary, and in *Dynamic Secularization* I had focused on two, both of which have remained active: Temple of the Jedi Order and The Jedi Church (Bainbridge 2017: 131–43). The Order has a very extensive website that included the texts of fully 743 sermons, as of November 29, 2023, a few of which have the early date of November 30, 1999.[25]

"Jedi Church (The original)" was founded in New Zealand, and in early 2023 was very excited about the upcoming national census which would ask the religious affiliations of their citizens. The 2001 census of England and Wales tallied 390,127 Jedi. There were also 70,509 Jedis in Australia, 21,000 in Canada, 53,000 in New Zealand, and 14,052 in Scotland.[26] Nations differ in whether they include religion among their regular census questions (Thorvaldsen 2014), and the English tradition has evolved to do so because some government funding is provided for social programs managed by churches, while separation of church and state has prevented a similar count in the United States. Widely shared email communications had stimulated people to say they were devoted Jedis in 2001, but how many were secular folk either joking or complaining about inclusion of religion in the census, we do not exactly know. The numbers have been lower in subsequent censuses, for example 20,409 in New Zealand in 2018. The Temple has a Facebook page with 10,000 followers, but apparently no public Facebook group. The Jedi Church does have a Facebook group that had 9,862 members when I first studied it in 2016, and 8,923 members eight years later.

---

[24] jedihistory.weebly.com/the-founders.html.   [25] www.templeofthejediorder.org.
[26] en.wikipedia.org/wiki/Jedi_census_phenomenon.

A primary source of information about the early years of the Jediism movement is a series of publications by Davidsen (2013, 2016, 2017, 2018), that among other results prepared the way for the World Religions and Spirituality Project to include fully fictional religions in its encyclopedia (e.g. Bainbridge 2020a). He distinguishes "between the self-identified Jedi Realists for whom the Jedi Path is a spiritual way of life, and the Jediists who seek to develop Jediism into a full-fledged and legally recognized religion" (Davidsen 2017:10). This Element offers extensive information about Jedi Realists, considering their subculture to be a parareligion, or even an unregistered folk religion if we consider California Zen to be one, and it includes fully religious Jediism, even as we may worry that pure Jediism may have faded in recent years. Davidsen's extensive 2017 article listed many Jedi websites that had already been shut down, often providing a link to where one was preserved at Internet Archive. In twenty cases, he was able to provide a direct link that was still active that year, but when I checked them in March 2024, ten had vanished and four were inactive. Interestingly, two of the six active groups were local and expressed clear evangelical missions:

> California Jedi strives to nurture the growth of its members, give back to the Jedi Community by supporting Jedi of quality and building training resources, and serve our communities through our path . . . A Jedi is someone who through their own will and spirit strives to be a stronger, better, and more helpful person to the world. Utilizing the truth in fiction, we strive to follow a path inspired by the fictional Jedi in Star Wars in our real lives.[27]

> At Chicago Jedi, we believe that the lessons of the Jedi are not limited to the fictional realm of Star Wars, but can be applied to our everyday lives. Through training and practice, we strive to develop our physical, mental, and spiritual abilities, and use them to serve our communities and make a positive impact on the world around us.[28]

A broad overview of the online Jedi community is provided by a census of Facebook groups devoted to *Star Wars*. I joined 28 of them, and occasionally quote from public ones. While Table 3 lists the clearly religious groups, Table 2 lists the fandom groups that were not explicitly religious, but that often contained spiritual and philosophical material, and whose memberships probably varied along a dimension from secular to sacred. Three specialized in players of particular computer games: SWTOR Players Club,[29] Star Wars Jedi: Survivor, and Star Wars Galaxies Legends community. I added descriptors in brackets to three of the names. The "costume role-play" group helps fans organize social

---

[27] californiajedi.org/about/mission-statement/.   [28] chicagojedi.com/.
[29] SWTOR stands for Star Wars: The Old Republic. See Section 7.

Table 2 Facebook groups that represent the Jedi subculture

Name	Year Born	Members	Posts in Month	Joined in Week	Type
The Mandalorian & Star Wars Universe	2019	407,214	2,840	1,290	public
Darth Vader Fans	2019	363,678	3,978	1,362	Public
Star Wars Memes	2015	355,457	659	142	Public
Star Wars Fans	2014	127,934	2,278	216	Private
Darth Vader: Long Live The Sith	2018	61,797	85	12	Public
The Force Is Strong With This Group	2013	52,378	184	6	Private
Star Wars Sith Acolyte	2020	36,558	144	82	Public
SWTOR Players Club	2014	16,657	205	17	Public
Star Wars Jedi: Survivor	2017	14,455	22	18	Private
Jedi Girls Cosplay [costume role-play]	2016	4,756	5	4	Public
The Jedi Order	2017	4,572	137	4	Private
Lords of the Sith	2011	3,946	31	1	Private
The Jedi Temple	2019	2,886	0	0	Public
Collectors of the Force [collecting]	2016	1,115	10	0	Private
Jedi Temple (Official) [spammed]	2010	1,037	39	1	Public
Star Wars Galaxies Legends community	2019	759	4	3	Public

gatherings where they are dressed like natives of the *Star Wars* galaxy. The "collecting" group is primarily devoted to displaying physical lightsabers, but across many groups the members share photographs of toys or art they possess or have created. The "spammed" group illustrates a sad end often suffered by Facebook groups that lose their administrators, because anybody is free to post advertisements or anything else, totally unrelated to the original theme of the group. Anyone who is registered with Facebook can see everything posted in a public group, but even for private groups non-members can see the numbers of members, posts in the past month, and new members in the past week, .

The groups are listed in descending order of their number of members on March 2, 2024, and the first with fully 407,214 is devoted to fans of a TV series, *The Mandalorian*, that launched in 2019 and continues to be in production, but does not seem to promote Jediism. The key character of the TV series is not a Jedi but a Mandalorian bounty hunter named Din Djarin who takes on the obligation to protect a tiny child named Grogu, who belongs to the same mysterious and unnamed species as Yoda and indeed possesses powers of the Force but cannot communicate Jedi ideology. The Mandalorians are a warrior organization like a religious order, but lacking connection with the Force, and who instead follow a very strict "Creed." Dramatized in episodes 17 and 18, membership requires a ritual dedication: "I swear on my name and the names of the ancestors . . . That I shall walk the Way of the Mand'alor . . . And the words of the Creed shall be forever forged in my heart. This is the Way. From this moment on, I shall never remove my helmet." Thus they are devoted warriors who suppress many human characteristics and are unwilling to say much about their faith: "One does not speak unless one knows."

During the month prior to March 2, 2024, 2,840 posts were added, a large absolute number but only 1 post per 143 members, correctly indicating that popular Facebook groups tend to be like open blogsites, where most members constitute an inactive audience. A good deal of administrator labor can be involved in managing a group, especially in controlling the behavior of members who are allowed to post. This group had six admins and twenty-seven moderators, and twenty-five of this thirty-three-person team were rated "top contributor" for adding frequent posts. This group warns members: "The Mandalorian rule in Facebook: Anything (positive, negative[,] etc.) that involves politics and/or religion, will no longer result in a strike. You will be REMOVED from the group. This also includes reaction gifs that contain political figures and/or religious content." A "strike" is a negative Facebook rating associated with removal of a post, while "reaction gifs" are images added as responses to posts. The exclusion of "religion" by this rule did not really prohibit abstract discussion of Jediism, and seemed to refer to critiques based on traditional religions, or just promotions of irrelevant faiths.

While the second largest group, Darth Vader Fans, shares photos of toys, costumes, cartoons, and screenshots from the movies, much of the material is artistically rather complex and even sophisticated. On March 3, 2024, a post asked: What do you believe drove Darth Vader to embrace the dark side? Within four hours, it received 454 comments, including some analyses like these:

> Fear and pain. Both of these emotions are the cause of anger. Unresolved anger becomes hatred. It's the same reason all of humanity is controlled by

the darkness. Humans were defeated long ago by evil. Skepticism and doubt still rule over the human soul. Humanity is actually far more powerful than any Jedi. The problem is that nobody has enough faith to realize it.

Being born into slavery on a desert planet. Leaving the only relative he ever had. The death of the Jedi that found him. The scorn of much of the Jedi Council. Adolescent feelings of love creating attachments. The death of his mother in his arms.

Fear of losing loved ones. His time with the Jedi began with losing Qui-gon. Ten years later, it was his mother he lost, after he had just found her. He was plagued by more visions of Padmé's death. He was so afraid of feeling that loss again that he allowed himself to become obsessed with saving her, no matter the cost. He ultimately became his own undoing.

Anakin is the typical "gifted child" who's praised and molded their entire childhood into a set career based on their skill set instead of personality or desires. He was taught to fear attachments and The Darkside so he simply hid it. Then throughout the war he witnesses the council repeatedly allow atrocities to be performed but refuse to act with haste because of laws he feels is lackluster and ancient.

Two of the private groups in Table 2 primarily share dramatic pictures related to *Star Wars*, rather than being explicitly religious, yet do include the competing Jedi and Sith principles in their self-descriptions that can be seen by nonmembers:

> The Jedi Order follows The Jedi Code:
> There is no emotion, there is peace.
> There is no ignorance, there is knowledge.
> There is no passion, there is serenity.
> There is no chaos, there is harmony.
> There is no death, there is the Force
>
> Lords of the Sith follow The Sith Code:
> Peace is a lie.
> There is only passion.
> Through passion, I gain strength.
> Through strength, I gain power.
> Through power, I gain victory.
> Through victory, my chains are broken.
> The Force shall free me.

the numbers of members in Table 3 are lower than those for the large fan groups, but the explicitly religious groups have other modes of communication, and being a member may be more meaningful. Many of the new religious movements studied by social scientists are rather small compared with standard denominations, for example at peak around 10,000 for The Children of God

Table 3 Explicitly religious Jedi Facebook groups

Name	Year	Members	Posts in Month	Joined in Week	Type
Jedi Church (The original)	2008	8,923	29	4	Private
The Sith – A Star Wars Religion	2010	3,022	9	2	Private
The Church of Jediism Members Assoc.	2008	2,844	1	0	Private
Unified Jedi	2015	2,816	15	1	Public
Temple of the Jedi Force	2007	1,267	0	4	Public
Secret Society Of The Sith, Temple Of Sithism	2015	1,123	0	0	Private
The Jedi temple	2015	769	1	0	Private
Order of the Grey Jedi	2007	617	1	1	Private
International Jedi Federation	2019	310	10	1	Private
The Jedi Praxeum	2019	237	4	0	Private
Jediism is a religion	2009	211	0	1	Public
JEDInsider	2022	115	4	0	Public
UK Jedi Church	2011	88	3	1	Public

(Borowik 2023: 10). Yet once somebody joins a Facebook group, there is no automatic process to remove them for inactivity, so the actual membership could be significantly lower in some of these cases. I did not formally join The Church of Jediism, so joining the Members Association group in Facebook was not available.

The first group does appear active, and its public description includes: "Jedi Church with many thousands of members worldwide … We have several admins and moderators in this Facebook group. Everyone volunteers their time to help keep out spam and keep the peace. This Facebook group is a place to share your ideas on what the force means to you, and to ask questions of the community." The public statement for the second group is rather intense: "The Sith believed that conflict was the only true test of one's ability, and so emphasized its importance. It was their belief that conflict challenged both individuals and civilizations, and so forced them to grow and evolve. They believed that the avoidance of conflict – like the pacifist teachings of the Jedi – resulted in stagnation and decline." The third and apparently inactive group, Church of Jediism, offers no self description, just a link to its website. There we encounter this entrepreneurial welcome:

For whatever reason you are here, or whatever place or galaxy far away you have come from, you are meant to be here. Nothing is random. The Force has drawn you here and we hope in a world that often feels conflicted you will join us to Become the Force for love, kindness, compassion, spirit and light. Start studying Jediism today with our book Become The Force! Jediism is a new philosophy supporting the idea of one all-powerful life energy Force that connects all living things in the universe together. Only by balancing our self-awareness with unity awareness in the Force we can find ourselves and discover our meaning and purpose. Jediists believe we are all interconnected and one with the universal life Force. INTELLIGENCE. CREATIVITY. SELF CONTROL. SUPERPOWER [capitalization, spelling, and punctuation as in the original].[30]

Reportedly, it was founded in 2007 or 2008 in Wales by Daniel Jones (Cusack 2010: 128), and the website primarily promotes his book *Become the Force* based on interviews he gave to Theresa Cheung, a prolific author herself whose website says her areas are "spirituality, dreams and the paranormal."[31] Its prologue makes an interesting claim: "Jediism is a digital philosophy. Followers embrace technology and regard the internet as an absolutely essential tool for spreading the word and connecting like-minded individuals. This means it can be practiced with the application of online technologies alone and requires no physical church or place of meeting for followers" (Jones 2017: xiii). That suggests that Jediism need not fully become a religion, however similar it may be in terms of its psychological functions or supernatural assumptions.

The rather active Unified Jedi group says it "is dedicated to help grow the Jedi Realist Community and Jediism movement, philosophy, and religious beliefs both online as well as in offline activities. Within the Jedi Community, we have plenty of Facebook groups, online forums and offline groups. Some of which play nice with each other and other parts well not so much." We noted "Jedi Realist" is widely used to describe people who apply the principles of Jediism in their real lives. Another online social world is Second Life, in which the user can create simulated environments (Farley 2017). The Second Life Star Wars Roleplay Wiki contrasts: "Jedi Realism is the concept of the more philosophical side of being a Jedi – in other words the Jedi mindset – as opposed to purely role-playing as a Jedi. To someone who believes or follows this path, it is more important that his or her actions are based on the teachings of the Jedi than simulating the look and talk of a Jedi. In other words it is more like being rather than seeming."[32] The one other active group in Table 3, International Jedi Federation, is also Realist, "the gathering of offline chapters and affiliates to

---

[30] www.becometheforce.com.   [31] www.theresacheung.com/.

[32] swrp.fandom.com/wiki/Jedi_Realism.

form a stronger organization. Inspired by the fictional Jedi in Star Wars, we choose to practice the Jedi Path as a way of life. We create a sense of community as we share our knowledge and resources with one another."

While the Facebook groups listed in Table 2 primarily serve an audience, without requiring any investment from them as would be the case for a client cult, we might have expected the apparently religious groups in Table 3 to show much more social activity. My overall impression is that some of the religious Facebook groups failed, perhaps losing active members to other groups, while some continued to be viable but used other media for active communication. Indeed, the dyad of a Jedi Master and a "Padawan," who is the student of the master, can be carried out well at a great distance over Zoom, which offers the advantage of live video, or even via email with occasional attachments.

4 A Vast Diversity of Scriptures

The *Star Wars* library is huge, including not merely novelizations of the movies and many creative works of fiction licensed within the franchise, but also about 54,400 works written by amateurs at FanFiction.Net and 224,390 at archiveofourown.org, as of January 27, 2024. This vast collection of imaginative literature can be described in many ways. Sociologist Neil Smelser (1962) would have described it as mild *collective behavior*, similar to a social movement yet less formally organized. A key concept in Smelser's theory is social-psychological *strain*, a concept often attributed to Robert K. Merton (1938), that may be described as the motivation felt by an individual who cannot succeed in achieving goals set by the wider culture through following its behavioral norms. In their influential theory article about why some people join radical cults, John Lofland and Rodney Stark (1965) begin with the strain theory concept that recruits must first "experience enduring, acutely felt tensions." A reader of one of the fanfiction stories temporarily departs to some extent from the trials and tribulations of mundane life, and vicariously experiences subjective rewards that Stark and I called *compensators*. The author typically had a much more intense escape from reality while writing the story, seeking and perhaps gaining a little real social status as a temporary leader with followers. Thus, the relationship between author and reader resembles that between a Jedi Master and a Padawan who is the student of the master. More technically stated, this huge *Star Wars* literary subculture is an impressive example of a *collective audience cult*.

The real leader of a comparable and competing subculture, J. R. R. Tolkien, the author of *The Lord of the Rings*, would offer a different analysis, defining the authors of fanfiction as *sub-creators*. The online encyclopedia, *Tolkien*

Gateway, explains that "a human author is a 'little maker' creating his own world as a sub-set within God's primary creation. Like the beings of Middle-earth, Tolkien saw his works as mere emulation of the true creation performed by God."[33] Truth may be what we truly believe, even if it is factually uncertain, and Samuel Taylor Coleridge (1817) urged *willing suspension of disbelief* rather than *belief* in art and mythology. Tolkien (2008: 52) himself famously philosophized about the near-truth of children's fantasy stories, explicitly rejecting Coleridge's concept: "What really happens is that the story-maker proves a successful 'sub-creator.' He makes a Secondary World which your mind can enter. Inside it, what he relates is 'true': it accords with the laws of that world. You therefore believe it, while you are, as it were, inside" (original punctuation).

Since the invention of writing, long-lasting and influential religions tended to identify some texts as authentic, while debating which others were at best apocryphal or even heretical. In the context of digital religion, Radde-Antweiler (2013: 89) emphasized that the term *authentic* can mean a situation when cultural elements, "for example particular beliefs and performances, are part of a given religious system." The current terminology within the *Star Wars* commercial sector calls authentic novels *canon*, and describes apocryphal novels as *legends* of which Wikipedia counts 25.[34] A decade earlier, the terminology was somewhat vague, referring to a vast diversity of products that explored beyond the immediate scope of the first six movies as the *expanded universe*. That changed after Disney purchased Lucasfilm. Wookieepedia explains that "the Expanded Universe would be rebranded as Legends and no longer adhered to; past tales of the Expanded Universe would be printed under the *Star Wars* Legends banner, and a new continuity would be established that consisted only of the original six films, *Star Wars: The Clone Wars*, and all future material from that point onward."[35] However, fanfiction authors do not interact directly with Disney and are able to define *canon* more broadly. There is something a little paradoxical about an official implication that some fiction is true, while other fiction is false, but then our beliefs about reality do leave room for doubt.

There is good reason to think that Jesus really existed two thousand years ago, certainly as the leader of a small religious group. Conceivably, Princess Leia Organa really existed a long time ago in a galaxy far, far away, but more likely she was a fictional character imagined by author George Lucas and brought to reality by actress Carrie Fisher. She unexpectedly died December 27, 2016, yet was resurrected in the 2017 movie, *The Last Jedi*, which was dedicated: "In loving memory

---

[33] tolkiengateway.net/wiki/Sub-creation.   [34] en.wikipedia.org/wiki/List_of_Star_Wars_books.
[35] starwars.fandom.com/wiki/Star_Wars_Legends.

of our princess, Carrie Fisher" (Derschowitz 2017). Fully 70,000 fans attended the 2017 *Star Wars* Celebration in Orlando, Florida, that especially gave tribute to the late Carrie Fisher.[36] In a panel celebrating 40 years of the subculture, her daughter, Billy Lourd, shared the sacredness of that moment:[37]

> No one could have known what this once little dream of a movie would eventually become and what it would mean to millions worldwide. Mostly not her. But in our world *Star Wars* ultimately became our religion, our family, and our way of life. And I wanted to be here with all of you because I know that many of you feel the same way. When she surrounded herself with fans at celebrations like this she never felt more at home. She could spend hours talking to people and learning about their lives and how *Star Wars* and Leia touched them the same way it touched us.

George Lucas provided the introduction, and these words of holy love were followed by John Williams conducting an orchestra that played the theme he had composed to represent Princess Leia. As musicologist Frank Lehman has fully documented, Williams applied Richard Wagner's *leitmotif* methodology, writing melodies to represent people and phenomena from the story, that would be integrated into the music when appropriate.[38] Indeed, Williams not only composed one for Leia, but also another for her relationship with Han Solo, as Callaway (2018: 72) suggested, "opening up interpretive possibilities that would otherwise remain inaccessible and, quite literally, unheard of." The Celebration also included a series of brief scenes from the movies, titled "A Tribute To Carrie Fisher," which by October 12, 2023, had earned 7,872,231 views and 15,741 comments, then placing this one first: "Carrie didn't pass away, she became one with the force [*sic*]." Among its 161 replies, these were highly liked by readers: "She has joined the cosmic force." "She really did. You'll see soon." "I have never in my life read a comment on YouTube that made me cry until I read this." "May she bond with us all through the force."[39] Around the time of the *Star Wars* Celebration, Gray (2017) published a novel titled *Star Wars: Leia, Princess of Alderaan*, which is a biography of her transition to adulthood, beginning at age 16, which may have inspired young female readers during their own years of maturation.

Religions have saints, and perhaps even goddesses, but also holy relics. An especially remarkable sacred toy is a 2004 rubbery statuette of Yoda who serves as anyone's Jedi Master. Press his left hand, and he proclaims in Yoda's voice: "The Force and its wisdom are all around us. Ask you will a Yes or No question.

---

[36] www.starwars.com/news/thank-you-for-an-amazing-star-wars-celebration.

[37] www.youtube.com/watch?v=YI5QodTtlME; www.insider.com/billie-lourd-carrie-fisher-star-wars-celebration-speech-2017-4.

[38] franklehman.com/starwars/.   [39] www.youtube.com/watch?v=sE99le5FBrY.

Sense the Force in my left hand. Press it and answer you I will." One may then ask many questions, pressing his left hand after each to get a random response. Some answers are definite, such as: "The answer you seek is yes." Others are ambiguous: "Difficult to see. Always in motion, the Force." Other somewhat rare answers are instructions for Master Yoda's student: "Clear your mind of questions. Only then the answer will you see."

A high-tech mass-produced artifact from the distant past of a galaxy far, far away is the "vault" that holds a copy of the *Book of Sith*, the Bible of the religious cult locked in mortal combat against the Jedi. It is about a foot wide and in the shape of a four-sided black pyramid, with a golden triangle on one side. Pressing that triangle makes the vault emit a grinding noise plus flashing red light, as one side lifts up and a drawer slides forward, holding the book. Dating from 2015, this edition has become rather costly. One very used Sith vault was for sale from eBay in March 2024 for $499, but the cost of a very good condition one was $1,149.90.

"Wild Power," a chapter in *Book of Sith*, supposedly by Mother Talzin, leader of the Nightsisters, is especially interesting: "My sisters, the galaxy has taken note of us, and the powerful will pay for our service. Our skills are superior, honed on the wild beasts of Dathomir" (Wallace 2015: 98). Talzin's scripture dismisses the simplistic concepts of Light and Dark side of the Force held by Jedi and Sith: "There is no need to separate what they call the living Force from the unifying Force. Both are manifestations of the Twin deities, and both are vibrantly, overwhelmingly alive" (Wallace 2015: 101).

There also exists a Jedi Bible, titled *The Jedi Path*, with its own very different vault. Interestingly, that book pretends to be a copy that originally belonged to Yoda but passed through the hands of many others before Luke Skywalker obtained it, and many of them added handwritten comments, such as Yoda's addition to the chapter about lightsabers: "Know themselves Padawans must, before a unique lightsaber they can build" (Wallace 2012: 61). All the text of a chapter titled "The Prophecy of the Chosen One" is illegible, as if each line had been turned black by a magic marker, and has this commentary by Luke Skywalker: "These pages were already defaced when the book came into my possession. I don't know who tried to suppress the prophecy, but it was most likely the Emperor" (Wallace 2012: 13).

Yet if one seeks creative scriptures about the Force, tens of thousands of them are free online, in the form of fanfiction stories. There are many ways to understand the role of *author* in modern culture, but when a text is based on a fantasy mythos already created by other authors, the word *plagiarist* may apply. Yet prior to industrialization, it was common for people to tell each other stories based on traditional plots and characters, without any sense of intellectual property laws. In the journal *Science,* I suggested that the Internet might return us to that liberating tradition in post-industrial society (Bainbridge 2003). So long as amateur authors publish *Star Wars* stories freely online without financial gain and often using pseudonyms, the Disney corporation may judge that any legal challenge would be difficult and could irritate its valuable fan base. The authors of fanfiction can develop some degree of social status and connect to each other in virtual friendships.

While only a few fanfiction writers may define their writings as parareligious, there is a sense in which they are all functioning as clergy giving sermons to their readers, whenever supernatural forces or moral issues feature in their stories. Also, writing about the actions of characters requires entering their minds, which is very analogous to operating an avatar in a computer game, now that authors tend to write on computers using word processors. Indeed, the *ecstatic transformation* concept proposed by Snodgrass may apply well, certainly whenever many hours of an author's consciousness are invested in a central character of a long work of literature.

Archiveofourown.org (AO3) is a good source for data about the popularity of characters in the works of fanfiction writers (Dym & Fiesler 2020). Table 4 assembles AO3 data from September 2022 into columns in terms of historical periods in the Jedi universe. The movies were created as three trilogies, the first telling the story of Luke Skywalker developing spiritual maturity, the second looking back at the life history of his parents, and the third trilogy set in his last years as a woman named Rey becomes the new Skywalker. The three other columns are in chronological order, assembling the events up to and including Luke's adventures: Rise of Empire, Clone Wars, Rebellion Era. These six categories are separated by Archive of Our Own, but some stories may be included in two or even more columns. Obi-Wan Kenobi was Luke's religious mentor, effectively sacrificing himself in the original 1977 film in a duel with Sith master Darth Vader, but he continued to guide Luke in the form of a supernatural spirit. In the prequel trilogy, young Obi-Wan interacted closely with Anakin Skywalker, who became Luke's father before morphing into Darth Vader and gaining a second row in the table.

We might have expected the original trilogy to have inspired the greatest number of fan works of literature, but 14,410 is far less than the 72,594 for the sequel, and two explanations do come to mind: (1) The sequels are very recent, and Rey became a Skywalker only in 2019, publicizing the mythos. (2) Given that the authors in Archive of Our Own tend to be women, they may have rejoiced that *Star Wars* had turned toward their gender. There is something mystical about the fact that Rey's chief antagonist for supernatural power was a man, Kylo Ren, who had turned toward the Dark Side of the Force, and

Table 4 Popularity of characters in separate *Star Wars* testaments

	Original Trilogy	Prequel Trilogy	Sequel Trilogy	Rise of Empire	Clone Wars	Rebellion Era
Stories in Category	14,410	28,991	72,594	53,981	35,947	32,176
Luke Skywalker	55.7%	9.6%	12.0%	6.6%	5.1%	27.7%
Leia Organa	45.5%	7.8%	21.5%	5.3%	4.0%	23.7%
Han Solo	36.1%	2.6%	10.8%	1.8%	1.2%	17.9%
Obi-Wan Kenobi	20.8%	69.6%	1.9%	53.1%	46.7%	11.7%
Darth Vader	13.3%	2.6%	0.4%	1.9%	1.4%	7.0%
Chewbacca	12.0%	1.1%	1.2%	0.8%	0.6%	5.8%
R2-D2	6.1%	2.3%	1.4%	1.7%	0.7%	3.1%
C-3PO	5.0%	1.6%	1.5%	1.0%	0.8%	2.5%
Anakin Skywalker	11.7%	47.5%	2.1%	37.7%	36.4%	6.8%
Padmé Amidala	9.5%	24.8%	1.3%	16.7%	13.5%	5.1%
Qui-Gon Jinn	3.1%	21.6%	0.3%	12.5%	4.9%	1.6%
Ahsoka Tano	7.9%	17.8%	0.8%	22.9%	31.6%	9.4%
Mace Windu	2.1%	11.6%	0.3%	8.6%	8.6%	1.5%
CC-2224	Cody	2.3%	11.5%	0.1%	17.4%	24.6%	1.8%
Yoda	5.0%	11.0%	0.6%	7.7%	6.8%	2.8%
CT-7567	Rex	3.8%	10.9%	0.2%	19.9%	28.7%	5.3%

Table 4 (cont.)

	Original Trilogy	Prequel Trilogy	Sequel Trilogy	Rise of Empire	Clone Wars	Rebellion Era
Rey	4.8%	2.1%	53.1%	1.4%	0.8%	3.1%
Poe Dameron	3.2%	1.1%	35.7%	0.8%	0.4%	2.5%
Armitage Hux	1.8%	0.7%	35.4%	0.5%	0.2%	1.2%
Kylo Ren	1.6%	0.7%	30.3%	0.4%	0.2%	0.9%
Finn	2.6%	1.0%	29.0%	0.7%	0.4%	1.9%
Ben Solo	2.0%	0.6%	14.4%	1.0%	0.1%	1.1%
Rose Tico	1.1%	0.5%	13.0%	0.3%	0.1%	0.8%

originally had been named Ben Solo. He was the son of Luke's friend, Han Solo, and of Luke's sister, Princess Leia Organa. Ben was the nickname or pseudonym of Obi-Wan Kenobi. Rey was apparently the daughter of insignificant commoners but learned that her father had been a clone of evil Emperor Palpatine, and renounced this heritage by becoming a Skywalker and taking on the role of savior that Luke had abandoned. Indeed, the Light Side of the Force seemed not exactly "good," but meditative and detached.

It is noteworthy, but perhaps a bit distressing, that the two droids, R2-D2 and C-3PO, were not very popular in the new scriptures. For each of the columns, the rows of the table were originally assembled from the 10 characters that AO3 initially listed. This duo had to be added later because one character was listed three times: Darth Vader, Anakin Skywalker, and their combination. The term "droid" is a contraction of "android," which means a robot that resembles a person, and indeed they had two very different personalities and were acted by people in the movies. Another character, slightly more popular, is tall and hairy Chewbacca, a member of the Wookiee species from the planet Kashyyyk, incapable of speaking a Human language and more violent than intellectual, but shown in the original movie as playing a videogame against R2-D2.

Two other popular characters are Ahsoka Tano and Yoda. Ahsoka is a Togruta from the planet Shili, who served as apprentice to Anakin Skywalker. A review by Brown (2023) of Ahsoka's new TV series reported: "Much like her master, the teenager was reckless, impulsive, stubborn and didn't always follow the rules. She was also the first female Jedi protagonist that audiences got to see in action on screen." Yoda is a non-human of uncertain ancient lineage who seemed to be the last Jedi Master, teaching, according to Wookieepedia: "the Jedi tradition to Luke Skywalker, and unlocking the path to immortality."[40] All other characters in the table are Human, despite the fact that the planet Earth does not exist in any "galaxy far, far away."

It would take a lifetime to read all these stories, let alone analyze the wide matrix of cultures they depict. For an example of AO3 scripture, we can consider *Remedial Jedi Theology*, written by someone using the pseudonym MarbleGlove, that consists of seven chapters with 51,336 words, thus qualifying as a book.[41] Since publication in 2018, by September 2022 it received 61,353 hits which are the equivalent of Wikipedia pageviews, 780 kudos by people rating it high, and 4,029 bookmarks by readers who planned to return to it. By January 28, 2024, the hits had risen to 65,905 and the kudos to 4,244, while the bookmarks had dropped to 2,203 after readers had finished.

---

[40] starwars.fandom.com/wiki/Yoda.
[41] archiveofourown.org/works/15118700/chapters/35054840.

Focused on the education of Obi-Wan Kenobi and Anakin Skywalker, it also includes Padmé Amidala, the mother of Luke Skywalker and Leia Organa, of whom Anikin was father before he became Vader. The author provided this background: "Let us consider the fact that the Jedi Order is a monastic religious organization based out of a temple, with five basic tenets of faith."

1: Death, yet the Force: "Once a being has existed they can never truly be gone, for the Force connects all living things through both space and time."

2: Chaos, yet Harmony: "Never assume that someone is acting irrationally just because you don't understand the rationale."

3: Passion, yet Serenity: "Jedi go into some of the most dangerous situations in the galaxy, often as lone individuals trying to overturn centuries of cultural conflict. We are demonized as often as we are idolized."

4: Ignorance, yet Knowledge: "When emotions don't leave us, it's because we haven't found the correct source of them. Until you find the source, it will return."

5: Heresy, yet Orthodoxy: "Once you have a winning streak, people are more likely to believe you next time. It gives people the impression that your word matters more."

An epilogue reconsiders the third tenet as Emotion, yet Peace: "Eventually all children, and adults too, must choose and then choose again, where their home is." A fellow member of AO3, using the name Talavin, wrote this comment: "It is extremely rare to read a fanfic that really captures the truth of the Jedi. So many people put their own perspectives as Westerners on it, and conclude that the Order's teachings on attachments are bad. Yours is one of two stories I can recall ever reading that really do the Jedi justice. I absolutely adore how you bring the jedi to life as a religious order dedicated to self sacrifice and balance." MarbleGlove replied to Talavin: "Thanks for the wonderful review! And okay, what was the second story that you recall that really did the Jedi justice?" Talavin replied that it was *A Legacy of Strength* by PadmeKSkywalker, published not in Archive of Our Own but in the earlier yet still popular FanFiction.net.[42] It had fully 175,434 words in 56 chapters and imagined that Darth Vader might possibly never have existed, given that the protagonist seems calm and happy by the last sentence: "The transformation of Anakin Skywalker was complete." Another member, Comet360, commented to MarbleGlove:

> I just want to add my support for your interpretation of Jedi theology. It's pretty obvious that Lucas borrowed heavily from Asian influences for the Jedi, where cultures often emphasize the needs of the community over the

---

[42] www.fanfiction.net/s/2622692/1/.

needs of the individual, and Buddhism has the whole letting go of everything philosophy ... I also really love the way you wrote the religious element of the Jedi. It was continually reinforced throughout the story that everything the Jedi learned, from lightsaber dueling to etiquette to not making attachments, was all so that they could better serve the will of the Force, emphasizing the religious motivation over the resulting diplomat warrior they become.

Every tale told by a fan adds some details to the existing mythos, but AO3's classification system allows authors to apply Alternate Universe tags, which might be considered heretical because they contradict one or more important officially accepted "truths." As of December 2, 2023, authors had tagged 20,353 stories in the Canon Divergence subcategory, implying they had creatively diverged in some significant ways. Another tag, Modern Setting was applied to 17,649 stories, implying they connected to our own world and did not date from "a long time ago." Those two subcategories overlapped in many cases, and with two smaller subcategories: College/University setting (2,058 works) and Everyone Lives/Nobody Dies (2,397 works). Table 5 maps the Alternate Universe by showing how popular characters were distributed across these creative subcategories, plus their connection to primary movie sources.

The term *canon* is widely used, both in fan fiction and the *Star Wars* community, to refer to the centrally defining components of the mythos, here the original and prequel trilogies. Not surprisingly, College/University seems to be a subcategory of Modern Setting, both connecting to the most recent trilogy of sequel movies. The movie *Rogue One* dates from 2016, was not part of a trilogy, and ended with the deaths of most heroic characters, inspiring fan authors to reject that outcome. Although the Disney corporation has the right to decide which products can bear the *Star Wars* trademark, the noncommercial authors lack a charismatic leader who could draw the line between canon and heresy, even as *charisma* often plays a key role in the institutionalization of a new religion. The history of computer games seems far more rule-based and raises serious questions about human freedom.

5 Virtual Worlds

Games based in the *Star Wars* mythos, especially the complex *virtual worlds* enabled by modern computers, take religiousness further, offering beyond audience cults the equivalent of *client cults* and providing new forms of communication for participants who might be open to participation in a complete religious movement.

Table 5 Character popularity in alternate universe stories of four types (Bold numbers highest in column)

Character	Canon Divergence	Modern Setting	College/ University	Everyone Lives / Nobody Dies	Primary Movie Source
Obi-Wan Kenobi	**7,825**	2,321	277	417	Prequel Trilogy
Anakin Skywalker	**5,455**	2,015	225	328	Prequel Trilogy
Luke Skywalker	**4,575**	2,347	286	305	Original Trilogy
Leia Organa	**4,349**	3,573	415	391	Original Trilogy
Ahsoka Tano	**3,625**	1,013	143	221	Clone Wars
Rey	3,425	**8,920**	**1,003**	134	Sequel Trilogy
Ben Solo | Kylo Ren	3,267	**7,818**	**916**	133	Sequel Trilogy
Armitage Hux	1,888	**4,942**	**605**	70	Sequel Trilogy
Poe Dameron	2,178	**4,930**	**695**	106	Sequel Trilogy
Finn	1,679	**4,408**	**605**	93	Sequel Trilogy
Cassian Andor	1,974	912	153	**1,331**	Rogue One
Jyn Erso	895	855	144	**1,197**	Rogue One
Bodhi Rook	486	507	88	**855**	Rogue One
Chirrut Îmwe	294	299	46	**529**	Rogue One
Baze Malbus	291	291	40	**528**	Rogue One

The economic strategy for nearly all massively multiplayer online games is to require either a monthly subscription or "free to play, pay to win" in which many simulated goods, abilities, and access to areas may be bought in-game using virtual currency that must be purchased for real-world dollars. Popular solo-player games usually just must be bought, but are released in a series over the years, thus comparable to a subscription but paying cash for each episode. For example, the online computer game store, Steam, sells fifteen games in the archaeological *Tomb Raider* series that was so popular it became a trio of movies. Client cults provide various services that have some similarity to religion, in that they provide a range of specific to general compensators under assumptions that are not empirically verified and resemble supernatural beliefs. Thus they are a parareligious form of business.

Earlier in the history of online games, some popular ones were based on conventional religion, such as *GodStoria: The Bible Online* which launched in 2010, but there also was widespread Christian concern that videogames taught bad values to young people (Bainbridge 2013). In her extensive analysis of religious expression in virtual reality, *Godwired*, Rachel Wagner (2012: 40) noted the problem that popular games often gave players a degree of freedom to shape the plot of the underlying story: "One can imagine that a game that allowed users to 'save' Jesus from the cross would not go over very well with many Christians." In technical terms, *GodStoria* was rather primitive and long since deceased, today giving a second meaning to its "Old Testament" setting. Creating popular computer games today is very costly, requiring an international audience, with many game companies operating from Japan and China where Christianity was never dominant. Indeed, a number of Asian games promote competitors to Christianity, as for example the popular 2005 Chinese game *Perfect World* which emphasizes Taoism.

On March 11, 2024, I entered the word "Christ" into the search system in Steam, and it tried to sell me four games based on the secular mystery novels by Agatha Christie, followed by *Christmas Massacre* described thus: "Christmas is coming and Larry's got a big problem – his Christmas tree is telling him to KILL! Lead him through his murder rampage." The first potentially Christian game in those search results was a simple one from 2016, *Jesus Christ RPG*, "where you can play as Jesus Christ and the Apostles in turn-based battles," that earned just 1,561 player reviews, compared with the 99,935 reviews earned by *Rise of the Tomb Raider* that launched the same year.

However, many abstract concepts in computer games are also found in the Bible and may have been derived from it, although significantly secularized. In a chapter about apocalyptic games, Wagner (2012: 187, 191) first mentions *Assassin's Creed*, which encourages players "to see themselves as messianic agents of deliverance against the forces of evil." Very popular, it grew into a series in which the player travels supernaturally back in time, again and again, to experience conflict between historically real religious movements, notably the Christian Templars versus the Islamic Assassins (Bainbridge 2023c: 55). The 2022 issue, *Assassin's Creed Valhalla*, has this theme: "Become a legendary Viking on a quest for glory. Raid your enemies, grow your settlement, and build your political power." It earned 18,203 Steam reviews, mostly positive. However, Steam does not describe *Assassin's Creed* as apocalyptic but as featuring historical combat. In contrast, Steam advertises fully 1,926 *post-apocalyptic* games, but generally the apocalypse was caused by nuclear war, as in the *Fallout* series, or a disease pandemic, rather than anything related to traditional faiths.

The *ecstatic transformation* concept was directly applied by Snodgrass (2023) to the psychological function performed by avatars in the massively multiplayer online subscription game, *World of Warcraft*, and the spiritual significance of playing a game may depend both upon its narrative and technical features. Early videogames based on *Star Wars* were very simple simulations of scenes from the movies, severely limited by the crude graphics and small memory of the devices. The first official release of one was in 1982, *The Empire Strikes Back* for the Atari 2600, which merely offered repetitive battle from a single scene of the 1980 film. Videos of early videogames can often be found on YouTube, for example 33 minutes of that one posted on a channel named Old Classic Retro Gaming that offers over a thousand such videos and had about 63,200 subscribers by November 24, 2023. The video had earned 8,152 views since it was posted September 27, 2021, and had this description "A horizontal shoot 'em up game where you are a pilot of a snow speeder fighting the imperial walkers on the icy planet of Hoth."[43] The graphics are very low resolution, just structures built from rectangles of uniform color, with "bang" sounds as the player's speeder fights tank-like walkers again and again, and the *Star Wars* melodic theme occasionally plays.

The 1992 *Super Star Wars* for the Super Nintendo requires players to try each scene multiple times to learn how to complete it successfully, and a 46-minute high-skill playthrough on the World of Longplays channel earned 638,366 views since it was posted on October 4, 2015.[44] Luke received his lightsaber and after action scenes also involving Han Solo and Chewbacca, while flying as Luke through the trench on the Death Star, the player hears the voice of Obi-Wan Kenobi: "Use the force, Luke!" The game ends with celebration of victory:

---

[43] www.youtube.com/watch?v=nwjFDQMmXf8.
[44] www.youtube.com/watch?v=NnsGbd8WMNg.

"And remember! The Force will be with you always!" This video received 735 comments from viewers, such as: "This is so nostalgic. It takes me back to the times before the prequels when Star Wars was still shrouded in mystery and excitement." "This game taught my generation tolerance to frustration: you don't beat this game; you learn how to dominate it, which takes time and lots of dying!" "I love watching these videos of old games, because they evoke an almost 'sixth sense'. A sense that really brings back all sorts of thoughts, feelings, memories, and sensations of when I was young in the 90's."

Thus, early games had emotional and even spiritual impact, but they were probably not capable of simulating religion. Over the three decades since *Super Star Wars* was published, a vast cosmos of videogames and computer games was created, often giving greater emphasis to ethical issues and the power of the Force. Many of them are today accessible from the online Steam store, and Table 6 lists the most popular of them. The complex Steam search system offers text-based reviews by experienced players with positive or negative ratings, and the figures date from August 6, 2023. The numbers of reviews written by players do suggest the relative popularity within the Steam user community, but not exactly the over-all popularity. For example, *The Force Unleashed* launched in 2008 for ultimately eleven different videogame and computer systems, and the PC version seems to have first been available from Steam in 2009. That online store launched in 2005 but emphasizing Windows computer games and not handling TV-connected videogame systems. Also, games vary in the extent to which they exist in non-game forms, and a novel was published in 2008 in connection with this game (Williams 2008).

The system also categorizes each game, listing the most popular "tag" descriptions. For example, Steam lists 916 games or expansion products as "souls-like" and includes five products in the Japanese *Dark Souls* series of games from which this term arose. Of the 916, the numbers sharing its three most popular "genre" tags are *action* with 750, *adventure* with 572, and RPG (role-playing game) with 441. The three most often "themes and moods" tags shared with souls-like were *fantasy* with 316, *atmospheric* with 291, and *dark* with 154. So Steam's tag system does function as a concept-based classification system, but based on the history of the computer game industry.

Three of the twenty games in Table 6 belong to the popular LEGO franchise of children's plastic blocks, and they emphasize puzzle solving including assembling equipment, while exploring a vast maze. Here are some additional definitions: co-op allows two or more players to cooperate as a team but not in combat with others; VR = virtual reality; sci-fi = science fiction; FPS = first-person shooter; MMORPG = massively-multiplayer online role-playing game; RTS = real time strategy.

Table 6 Twenty popular *Star Wars* games available from Steam

Title = Star Wars +	Year	Reviews	Positive	Tag Descriptions
Jedi: Survivor	2023	34,251	62.6%	action, adventure, singleplayer, souls-like
LEGO: The Skywalker Saga	2022	38,805	91.6%	LEGO, adventure, multiplayer, co-op, space
Squadrons	2020	24,267	67.9%	flight, space, multiplayer, VR, sci-fi, action
Jedi: Fallen Order	2019	130,746	89.2%	action-adventure, third person, souls-like, action
Battlefront II	2017	50,325	87.4%	multiplayer, shooter, singleplayer, action, FPS
The Old Republic	2011	54,081	89.9%	free to play, multiplayer, MMORPG, open world
LEGO: The Clone Wars	2011	7,106	94.8%	LEGO, action, adventure, local co-op, co-op
The Force Unleashed II	2010	6,399	62.4%	action, singleplayer, hack and slash, sci-fi
The Force Unleashed	2009	9,224	73.9%	action, hack and slash, singleplayer, sci-fi
LEGO The Complete Saga	2009	21,009	96.6%	LEGO, local co-op, adventure, co-op, action
Empire at War – Gold Pack	2006	32,616	97.5%	strategy, RTS, space, sci-fi, multiplayer, 4X
Republic Commando	2005	14,193	95.7%	FPS, action, tactical, sci-fi, singleplayer
Knights of the Old Republic II	2005	21,818	93.5%	RPG, story rich, sci-fi, singleplayer, classic
Battlefront 2 Classic	2005	49,917	94.4%	action, multiplayer, shooter, classic, sci-fi
Battlefront	2004	3,620	96.5%	action, multiplayer, classic, FPS, sci-fi
Jedi Knight II – Jedi Outcast	2003	4,218	91.3%	action, classic, sci-fi, FPS, multiplayer
Jedi Knight – Jedi Academy	2003	12,300	96.1%	action, sci-fi, third person, multiplayer, classic
Knights of the Old Republic	2003	28,532	91.1%	RPG, sci-fi, story rich, singleplayer, classic
Galactic Battlegrounds Saga	2001	3,693	91.6%	strategy, RTS, action, multiplayer, singleplayer
Dark Forces	1995	2,699	89.5%	FPS, action, classic, sci-fi, shooter, retro

Wikipedia defines another: "4X (abbreviation of Explore, Expand, Exploit, Exterminate) is a subgenre of strategy-based computer and board games."[45]

Here we shall consider how religion was treated in *Star Wars Jedi Knight – Jedi Academy* and *Star Wars Jedi: Fallen Order*, released 16 years apart but both oriented to training an individual to become a Jedi Master. Both were of high quality for their year and both also require the player to follow set paths through a limited geography. The game centered on Jedi Academy seems to be an educational course introducing the Jedi universe, as its description in the Steam store says: "Take on the role of a new student eager to learn the ways of the Force from Jedi Master Luke Skywalker. Interact with famous Star Wars characters in many classic Star Wars locations as you face the ultimate choice: fight for good and freedom on the light side or follow the path of power and evil to the dark side."[46] Especially relevant here is that the game has a well-defined story about religious conflict, although it begins in total mystery that only gradually becomes clear.

The Jedi have long been at war with the Sith, following the Light Side versus the Dark Side of the Force. Thousands of years ago, with vastly powerful magic, Marka Ragnos became the Dark Lord but proved mortal, and was trapped in his tomb. The player takes the role of Jaden Korr, beginning by deciding which species and gender that Jedi student should be. Human male or female are both choices, but four species are gender determined, Twi'lek and Zabrak as female, Rodian and Kel Dor as male. Many scenes are like pieces of theater, so either a male or female voice actor will speak on behalf of the player, using the same script. The narrative is structured as a couple of dozen separate field assignments that start at the Jedi Academy. As Jaden completes missions, he or she gains magical skills using the Force, including these as described in the game's instructions:

Drain: "Allows Jedi to transfer a person's life essence to him or herself."

Lightning: "This dark side power hurls a devastating electrical attack against enemies."

Absorb: "When activated: this light side Force power will take damage from ... Drain and Lightning attacks and turns that energy into Force power for the Jedi to use."

Speed: "When activated, this Force power slows down the world around the Jedi, allowing him or her to gain a speed advantage over enemies."

Sense: "Allows Jedi to see enemies (including cloaked enemies), friendly characters, pickups and some world objects more clearly, even through walls."

---

[45] en.wikipedia.org/wiki/4X.

[46] store.steampowered.com/app/6020/STAR_WARS_Jedi_Knight__Jedi_Academy/.

Rage: "Affords Jedi protection against damage, an increase in speed, and an increase in damage potential, all at the expense of the Jedi's health."

After battles on many planets, the climax comes when Jaden Korr confronts Tavion Axmis who proclaims: "You're too late. Soon, Marka Ragnos will return and obliterate the Jedi. The Sith shall rule again!" Jaden nears victory, but then Tavion completes the resurrection of Ragnos, who enters her body to give her greater power, shouting "I shall not be denied!" Yet if Jaden destroyed the Scepter of Ragnos, the evil Lord will remain in his tomb for all eternity.[47] However, as in a few other *Star Wars* games, the player could choose to go to the Dark Side, in which case Jaden tries to steal the Scepter of Ragnos and use it to become a dictator.[48] Writing "Jaden Korr: Sith Empress," in Archive of Our Own, LenoraLana imagined what followed:

> Jaden Korr walked about on the Star Destroyer, ready to kill anyone who showed her the slightest disrespect. Tavion was dead, killed by her own hand, and she held the Scepter in one hand, her lightsaber in the other. She proceeded toward the bridge, for the most part ignoring the stares of all those she passed. Obviously people were wondering who she was, but probably assumed her to be one of Tavion's followers – an assumption she would correct as she entered the bridge. She was taking over, and she would be the leader of the Sith now. She had defeated her own master, and she would prove herself to be stronger than any other Dark Jedi.[49]

Steam's description of *Star Wars Jedi: Fallen Order* suggests a narrower narrative: "An abandoned Padawan must complete his training, develop new powerful Force abilities, and master the art of the lightsaber – all while staying one step ahead of the Empire."[50] Initially developed for PlayStation and Xbox One videogame systems, as well as Windows computers, it is an action-oriented game that emphasizes development of manual and mental skills, rather than philosophy. Indeed, the page on Steam that sells the game urges players to use a game controller rather than keyboard: "Jedi: Fallen Order delivers the fantasy of becoming a Jedi through its innovative lightsaber combat system – striking, parrying, dodging – partnered with a suite of powerful Force abilities you'll need to leverage to overcome obstacles that stand in your way."[51] The narrow story takes place five years after defeat of the Jedi by the Empire, and concerns a socially isolated Jedi Padawan named Cal Kestis, who must develop his abilities and bring together former Jedis and Force-sensitive children, in order

---

[47] www.youtube.com/watch?v=ns8LEz0H8Iw.
[48] www.youtube.com/watch?v=I4bZogrbYmA.
[49] archiveofourown.org/works/21375052/chapters/50917303
[50] store.steampowered.com/app/1172380/STAR_WARS_Jedi_Fallen_Order/.
[51] store.steampowered.com/app/1172380/STAR_WARS_Jedi_Fallen_Order/.

to restore the Fallen Order. Unable to achieve this lofty goal, Cal continues his adventures in the sequel, *Star Wars Jedi: Survivor*, that launched five years later.

It is possible that playing difficult, action-oriented videogames develops neural or cognitive abilities that might transfer to real world activities, but these particular games do not seem to promote Jedi religion as such. What happens at the end of the game? The player can play it again but at a higher level of difficulty, given development of the skills to do exactly that. In the Academy game, these are the four levels of difficulty choices when starting to play: Padawan, Jedi, Jedi Knight, and Jedi Master. There are also four in the Order game: Story Mode, Jedi Knight, Jedi Master and Jedi Grand Master. *Fallen Order* does offer occasional spiritual experiences. The first takes place immediately after Cal is rescued by former Jedi Cere Junda and alien pilot Greez Dritus whose Latero species had good manual skills given they possessed four arms. Resting for a few minutes, Cal casually begins playing Cere's guitar improvisationally, and she comments: "That song . . . I wrote it. Years ago. You touch an object and witness events connected to it. You feel its history." Later, while exploring the first planet, Cal touches another object and the player gets this message: "Through a rare ability known as Psychometry, Cal can receive information from the Force when he touches certain items."

In my early study of The Process polytheistic religious movement, I observed extensive psychometry rituals in which a person read psychic meaning from an object, and concluded it was a form of *directed fantasy* that can "have the effect of liberating the reader from excessive inhibitions and encouraging him to express himself" (Bainbridge 1978: 200). Over a century ago, there were serious debates over whether psychometry was a religious phenomenon, used a natural psychological ability, or belonged to the Spiritualist fad of that time (Trowbridge 1908). The Process used it as a recruitment technique in its weekly Telepathy Developing Circle that was open to early-stage clients, since pairs of participants would take turns practicing psychometry on each other. That meant holding to one's forehead an object that belonged to the other person, and reading the partner's magic aura from it, thereby building the beginnings of a social bond uniting the couple and drawing them into the core religion. Thus, the diversity of games and other components of the *Star Wars* mythos may be supportive of religious development, but performing different functions, some of which may be very personal. Other components are far more social.

6 Two Denominations

In the year 2003, two very different computer games took Jedi religion in new social directions. *Star Wars: Knights of the Old Republic* (KotOR) was a primarily solo-player game available for videogame systems as well as computers, structured rather like a sophisticated work of literature and including dramatic scenes that depicted conversations of many types with pre-programmed non-player characters. In the sense of the original Latin noun, "religio," it strongly mentors players about conscientiousness, sense of right, moral obligation, and duty, despite the lack of deities. Thus, it qualifies as religion for its ethics, which seem transcendent if not supernatural.

Star Wars Galaxies (SWG) was a massive multiplayer virtual world for computers where users may have multiple avatars, either to undertake pre-defined adventures or to create their own homes and communities, while interacting however they wished with other players. *Star Wars Galaxies* did not directly promote Jediism, or religious perspectives in general, but players were free to create their own private communities following the supernatural principles they themselves selected. A novel based on SWG emphasizes the challenge of knowing whom to trust in a world beset by conflict, and when retrieving lost information can determine the fate of civilization (Whitney-Robinson and Blackman 2004). In December 2011, galactic conflict became very real when SWG was closed down to make room for a competing virtual world, *Star Wars: The Old Republic*, a successor to KotOR, that will be the topic of the following section.

Theologically, KotOR connects to a concept in *The Phantom Menace* that we have already encountered: Balance. Anakin Skywalker and his mother were slaves, and Jedi Master, Qui-Gon Jinn, purchased the boy not to liberate him, but under the theory he would be valuable to the Jedi because of his high concentration of magical midi-chlorians, nor did he liberate the boy's mother. In a meeting with the Jedi Council, Qui-Gon endorsed an uncertain prophecy that an unusual Jedi might be the Chosen One who could bring balance to the Force, and proposed that Anakin must be trained to manage his powerful supernature.

As mentioned earlier, midi-chlorians were added to the mythos in *The Phantom Menace*, and one possible explanation is that giving a pseudo-biological, science fiction explanation for the Force could reduce the chance that traditionally religious members of the audience would react negatively, conceptualizing the Force as some kind of pagan deity. Yet there is another meaning that might magnify the religious quality of Jediism. Like the Virgin Mary, Anakin's mother in the movie claimed he did not have a father. Indeed, one of the problems faced by Jedi was that they must be celibate monks, as remains true for confirmed priests in the Roman Catholic Church. Yet as Anakin's son, Luke Skywalker, illustrates, if a Jedi Knight produces a child, it will likely have inherited greater than average midi-chlorians that strengthen the connection to the Force. So, Qui-Gon may have hoped that Anakin could find a way to love a woman, such as Padmé Amidala, and produce Jedi children with her without becoming dangerously selfish.

Knights of the Old Republic is set in the ancient history of the *Star Wars* galaxy, about 4,000 years before the events in the movies, when the Republic battles the Sith Empire, and each planet has a different society. The player enters by creating an avatar, giving it a name, and selecting gender, although for simplicity the publications about KotOR assume "he" was a male, and the differences in the story are minor.[52] Also at creation, one of three preliminary skill classes must be selected. The instructions on Steam describe them, each having its own values embodied with different algorithm variables:

> Scoundrels survive through wit and guile, traits that sometimes place them on the wrong side of the law. Intelligence, Dexterity and Charisma are the trademarks of a scoundrel.
>
> Scouts are explorers, trained to understand their surroundings and how to survive in them. Dexterity, Intelligence and Wisdom are the most important abilities of a scout.
>
> Soldiers are masters of combat in all its forms, believing that the best way to survive a fight is to win it. Dexterity, Constitution and Strength are key to an effective soldier.

Remarkably, the avatar lacks personal memories, and discovering his real identity is a hidden quest that becomes increasingly important as the hours pass. After completing introductory training in the technology of the software, the avatar can then adopt one of three classes of Jedi:

> Guardian . . . battles against the forces of evil and the dark side. They focus on combat training and masterful use of the lightsaber.
>
> Consular . . . seeks to bring balance to the universe. They focus less on physical combat and more on mental disciplines in order to augment their mastery of the Force.
>
> Sentinel . . . ferrets out deceit and injustice, bringing it to light. They strike a balance between the physical and mental disciplines of the Jedi Order.

A rather thorough "walkthrough guide" for playing KotOR on the website of Imagine Games Network (IGN) explains that a vast number and variety of decisions must be made "in your actions and in speaking with other characters, NPCs and otherwise."[53] Around 2003, many games involved strategic or tactical decisions, and alternative ethical consequences, probably for two reasons: (1) The electronic game industry was developing rapidly, so many early adopters of the systems were intellectual explorers, and (2) The graphics technology did not yet facilitate rapid movement that later prioritized quick player action rather than thoughtful analysis. The Wikipedia page for KotOR

---

[52] starwars.fandom.com/wiki/Star_Wars:_Knights_of_the_Old_Republic.

[53] www.ign.com/wikis/star-wars-knights-of-the-old-republic/Endar_Spire.

correctly states: "It was nominated for numerous awards and is often cited as one of the greatest video games ever made."[54] To begin with, it depicts a complex network of social relations between multiple characters, giving the player as many as nine secondary avatars, any two of which can undertake adventures in partnership with the primary avatar, plus dozens of well-defined non-player characters (NPCs). There are many multi-step conversations, in which the player can select among different responses from the avatar, in combined word count in the range of novels rather than theater dramas. The practical value of this complexity is that the player can be motivated to play the game many times, taking different decisions, yet completion is never quick, taking 50 hours or more the first time.

Hour by hour, the player learns more about the avatar's past and the nature of the apparently equal competition between Jedi and Sith. Eventually the story consolidates on the goal of killing Darth Malak, the Dark Lord of the Sith, which requires first gaining information from several planets about the location of the Star Forge military equipment factory that must be destroyed along with Malak. Before leaving the starter planet, Taris, the avatar rescues a Jedi Master named Bastila, or she rescues him given that they argue often about the nature of reality, and she becomes one of the secondary avatars called *companions*. To begin with, the avatar tells her he saw a vision when they met, in which she was fighting an enemy who may have been Revan, the previous Dark Lord of the Sith whom Malak replaced. Bastila begins to train the avatar to become a Jedi and tells him his own natural Force ability must have been strengthened temporarily by hers. In the background is a very different truth that takes many hours for the avatar to learn: the avatar is really Revan himself, and the Jedi may have erased his memory in order to use him against Malak.

Much of the intellectual content and many decisions that influence the course of the narrative are centered in conversations, usually between the player's avatar and a significant non-player character. Here is an example that initially seems merely to be encouraging the avatar to learn about the Force, yet has multiple deeper meanings. As the avatar is walking around the Jedi Enclave on the planet Dantooine, a woman named Belaya calls out: "You there! Padawan! Why are you not wearing the customary robes of the Jedi? Do you mock the honored traditions of our Order?" The player selects one of three responses from the avatar, seeking information or expressing polite or impolite reactions: (1) "Are you a Jedi?" (2) "I believe you are mistaken." (3) "Back off!" Belaya has correctly perceived that the avatar was already strong with the Force, and if the avatar mentions Bastila in their conversation, she comments: "Bastila? I have

---

[54] en.wikipedia.org/wiki/Star_Wars:_Knights_of_the_Old_Republic.

heard of her. They say she has already mastered the art of Battle Meditation, remarkable in one so young. Though I have heard she has a foolish pride in her own talents." In a later chance meeting, she offers mentoring advice to the avatar: "With power comes responsibility, and only by learning discipline and sacrifice can we truly learn to master our potential." To this point, Belaya seems merely like a minor mentor of Jediism, but she is also an instrument for rising doubts about the honesty of the Jedi Council and of Bastila, as well as being a character in an interesting side-story.

Later, the avatar is sent by Zhar, Revan's primary mentor and a member of the Jedi Council, to remove the taint from a corrupted grove, where Revan encounters an angry female with Force powers, who proclaims; "I am Juhani, and this is my grove. This is the place of my dark power. This is the place you have invaded. When I embraced the dark side, this was where I sought my solace. It is MINE!" In the past, she had been Belaya's closest friend, even with some implication the two Jedi women had been lovers. Yet love is not appropriate for Jedi, who must avoid passion. The Wookieepedia article for Juhani's mentor, Quatra, reveals that Jedi deception had caused tragedy:

> Juhani, a Cathar, had much trouble controlling her emotions and finding peace within herself. Master Quatra devised an unorthodox plan to test her Padawan's spirit. During a lightsaber training duel, Juhani failed her master's test. She lashed out in anger during their training session and struck Quatra down. Though Quatra only received minor wounds, she feigned death in order to test Juhani even more. Filled with fear and guilt at the 'death' of her master by her own hands, Juhani fell to the dark side and fled the Enclave, intent on never returning.[55]

The avatar has two companions and easily overpowers Juhani. They begin a very difficult conversation, in which the player gets a series of choices between different things to say. The player can decide to kill Juhani or save her, but her death is preordained if at any point the avatar selects the wrong choice, such as attempting to use the Jedi power to persuade using the Force. If the avatar gives the right responses, Juhani can safely return to the Jedi and perhaps also to Belaya. This is significant for the general story, because Juhani would then become a second Jedi companion for Revan, alongside Bastila. Otherwise, she would die.

A third one of the nine possible companions, Jolee Bindo, was a Jedi who experienced deep emotional conflict that caused him to abandon the Order and become a hermit on the planet Kashyyyk, the home world of the Wookiees including Chewbacca. Jolee's wife, "like many other Jedi, fell to the dark side. She attempted to turn Bindo, who resisted, culminating in a vicious lightsaber

---

[55] starwars.fandom.com/wiki/Quatra.

duel, which brought her to her knees. Unable to kill his own wife, Bindo let her go; this would ultimately lead to the deaths of many Jedi at her hands before she was finally struck down in battle."[56] At one point, Bastila argues with Jolee Bindo about why he has not officially returned to the Jedi. He asserts: "The capacity for good or evil, like the Force itself, is in all living creatures. And belonging to the Jedi Order, or the Sith, or any group, won't change what you are at your core."

So, who was Bastila at her own core? Much later, in an inconclusive first battle, Malak takes Bastila. Did she become Malak's prisoner, or his ally? When Revan next meets her, she is Malak's willing assistant. Yes, Revan must defeat Malak, but can that be done in performance of the Jedi mission or to return to the earlier status of Dark Lord of the Sith? One may imagine that either way Bastila could then play the role of Revan's wife and the mother of their supernatural children, assuming the avatar was the male version of Revan.

Clearly, *Knights of the Old Republic* is a virtual revolution that not only views ethical decisions as problematic, but gives equal honor to the Dark Side, which might remind us of the so-called Satanism scare of decades ago (Richardson, Best & Bromley 1991). Perhaps ironically, this gives much greater emphasis to the Jedi religion than do all the Disney movies and TV series of recent years. As a Steam reviewer who had played the game for 64 hours wrote:

> All of the praise you hear about this game is absolutely true . . . Playing through KotOR, it made me realize just how underwhelming the sequel trilogy really is. When writers are able to put together a story with so many interesting characters, so much philosophical discussion, and actual literary themes, it absolute boggles the mind that a massive studio like Disney cannot accomplish the same thing. Every character you encounter is interesting. Every planet you travel to has a well-defined political structure and unique problems that must be solved, without ever making things feel like busywork. Most can be accomplished in various ways, whether trying for a peaceful resolution, or just bursting in, guns and lightsabers blazing. You can hack computers, reprogram robots, and blow up power conduits to kill enemies, all while balancing light and dark-side leanings based on your choices in the story.

Star Wars Galaxies gave far less emphasis to the Force, but allowed each avatar to belong to the Republic, the Empire, or remain neutral, without any secondary avatars but intensely social (McCubbin 2005; McCubbin, Ladyman & Frase 2005). Since its launch in 2003, it had gone through many changes before I first explored it, beginning December 20, 2008. In stages, I created four main avatars and played each all the way to the maximum experience level of 90, plus three low-level avatars, continuing the participant observation through one or another

---

[56] starwars.fandom.com/wiki/Jolee_Bindo.

for 618 hours, and saving data in the form of 11,357 screenshot photos of the computer display. Massively multiplayer online games offer many opportunities to collect statistical data for use in social science, and conversations with both non-player characters and the avatars of other players can serve as interviews. Yet, as with real-world new religious movements, participant observation is often essential, giving the researcher the direct experience of the virtual reality (Festinger, Riecken & Schachter 1956; Becker and Geer 1957; Bainbridge 1978; Baker 1987), especially if multiple avatars explore the world in different ways, thereby reducing personal bias. Researchers must follow ethical principles in data collection, which is facilitated somewhat by the fact players only seldom reveal their actual identities.

At that point in the history of the galaxy, a new avatar needed to belong to one of ten species, including Human as well as nine kinds of alien, and to one of twelve professions. *Star Wars Galaxies* used professions to encourage players to perform different functions on a team, and to earn subscription income from players by encouraging each to create multiple avatars and thus enjoy more varied experiences over a period of years. *Star Wars Galaxies* gave great emphasis to living on simulated planets, building homes and villages, so four of the professions were *traders* with these specialties: domestics, engineering, munitions, and structures (Bainbridge 2010: 65–8).

My first avatar was an engineering trader who chose to remain neutral, thus potentially doing business with players belonging to both the Rebels and the Empire. The SWG wiki specified that this profession "specializes in high tech engineering including the construction and modification of droids, flight computers, cybernetics, vehicles, and electronics components. Engineers can also create weapon skill enhancing attachments and powerups through reverse engineering."[57] My second main avatar followed the Jedi profession and enthusiastically joined the Rebel faction. Each avatar began neutral, but could do missions for one faction or the other, to earn a positive reputation that was required for membership. It was possible to abandon membership, either to become neutral again or to work toward membership in the competing faction. Both of these initial avatars were female Humans, and my third was a male Human with the spy profession and membership in the Imperial faction.

For contrast, my fourth main avatar was a Wookiee, the hairy alien species to which Chewbacca belonged in the original movies. I named him Guzzlebooze in recognition of the fact that Chewbacca was the nickname Han Solo had given his fuzzy friend, since he liked to chew tobacco. At the point of assigning a profession to a new avatar, the SWG interface described Guzzlebooze's

---

[57] swg.fandom.com/wiki/Trader_(Engineering).

entertainer profession: "What cantina would be complete without a stellar band on stage and a dancer or two gyrating to the music? All the fame of top musicians and dancers can be yours! Top entertainers can inspire people to do their best, allow them to relax and enjoy a drink at the bar, or give them an internal rhythm to follow throughout their day." Note that some of the professions might seem to have magical powers, but SWG conceptualized entertainer psychologically, and medic biologically: "Medics use the powerful healing properties of bacta to keep others alive before, during, and after combat. Their remarkable knowledge of anatomy and medicines allow them to counter the detrimental effects of toxins, diseases, and vertigo."

Indeed, the emphasis of *Star Wars Galaxies* was to give people a more-or-less realistic experience of living on other planets, without encouraging supernatural beliefs that might be central to a Jedi religion. The user interface seemed to base the Jedi profession on the science of physics: "Jedi are Force Sensitive beings that can use their Force power to over-come and control their enemies and can master the art of fighting with a lightsaber. Force Sensitive individuals feel a connection to the energy that surrounds all living things and binds the galaxy together."

In its original form, SWG did not give players the option to select the Jedi profession when creating an avatar, and only a few months after its launch was it possible to earn Force sensitivity. One obvious concern was that players might all want to be Jedi, could use the Force to zoom across the galaxy and reach the maximum experience level, then use hyperspace to leave SWG for some other popular game and stop paying SWG's subscription. On November 15, 2005, the New Game Enhancements did allow starting an avatar as a Jedi, which was controversial with players, and in combination with other unpopular changes, the NGE caused a decline in active players, from about 250,000 to just over 100,000 (Olivetti 2015). On March 15, 2006, two Internet servers located in Japan were shut down, and twelve of the remaining twenty-five worldwide servers were subsequently closed on October 15, 2009.

Early in July 2011, I did a census of avatars in four of the thirteen then-existing Internet server versions of SWG, by entering each ten times, using the interface system that allowed searching for avatars that were currently active, then copying all the names and relevant data to spreadsheets. Of a total 2,848 avatars, 52.1 percent were Human, and 29.3 percent were Jedi (Bainbridge 2016: 71). I had not focused on faction membership in those data, but have saved the screenshot images, so for this publication I recopied the data for the 564 avatars on the server named Chilastra, finding that 244 were Rebels, 188 Imperial, and 132 neutral. The fractions Jedi were 29.5, 28.7, and 16.7 percent. That is consistent with the fact that time and effort were required to gain membership in a faction, but reveals no significant difference in the popularity of Jedi within the two factions. A total of 110 avatars belonged to one of the four manufacturing trader professions, but with 42 of them neutral, compared with 36 Rebels and 32 Imperials.

At the end of 2011, *Star Wars Galaxies* was shut down to make room in the marketplace for a new virtual galaxy which I immediately entered and have by now invested 1,194 hours of participant observation, *Star Wars: The Old Republic*. The last week of SWG was quite frantic, as great numbers of players rushed back to experience the galaxy one final time, and I myself took fully 1,751 screenshots December 10–16 across many group gatherings. The end was like a self-funeral, at which dozens of people dramatized their own virtual deaths, at Mos Eisley spaceport on the planet Tatooine. Some avatars were cursing the evil owners of the *Star Wars* franchise who decided to transfer the rights for a virtual world to a different company with new technology that might earn more money. One warned: "Brace for impact!" Another hoped they could all be reunited in *The Old Republic*: "See you in TOR!" Another expressed emotion: "Love you all." And a Force-sensitive avatar reported: "I feel a great disturbance in the force like a million voices screaming and were suddenly silenced!" Then a message from the game designers was displayed near the top of the screen: "RIP SWG. You had a long road and a ton of memories. People can hate all they want . . . but we love you . . . You will be disconnected in 10 sec so the server can perform a final save before shutting down. Please find a safe place to log out now." The system itself then briefly displayed: "Connection to SWG lost!"

A gradual miracle ensued, as a revivalist sect of mysterious hackers were able to launch several emulation servers over the following years, that allow a small number of SWG fans to continue playing. As of January 2024, it was still possible to access a YouTube video that was posted a decade earlier, showing people who were not already experienced in *Star Wars Galaxies* how to create an avatar and interact with the software and other avatars. It earned 418,957 views and 802 written comments, including: "I would just like to point out that as of Dec 16, 2011 the SWG client has been categorized under the DMCA exemptions clause as abandonware, thus it is NOT piracy to torrent the client."[58] Before translating this exotic language, we must note that the claimed legal status may be wrong. If the game player, or client, purchased the computer disks for *Star Wars Galaxies*, the client may not be violating any law to continue to play, even after SWG was removed from Internet. But the software cannot work without connection to an Internet server linked to other players and having

---

[58] www.youtube.com/watch?v=7tBjP4rpDhI.

its own software and data. *Abandonware* is software no longer provided commercially; *torrent* means to share many large files online; and *DMCA* refers to the painfully complex Digital Millennium Copyright Act. As in the case of the *Star Wars* fanfiction at Archive of Our Own, original publishers may decide not to sue for copyright or trademark violation, which could anger fans, but they may have the right to do so. Among the consequences are that the SWG emulators generally do not charge money for their services, although they may accept voluntary contributions. Also they tend to keep secret their locations and the real names of their staff members.

One list indicated there were fully twenty-five "rogue servers" offering SWG (Crosby 2022), although some may have been versions of each other, and some very incomplete. They tended to begin with only part of the original contents, after which the most popular ones began adding new material of their own creation. An enthusiastic but realistic appraisal of *Star Wars Galaxies* was offered by experienced game journalist, Bree Royce (2023), who first explored it when it launched in 2003: "There simply is no MMORPG or sandbox in existence that does what SWG does as well as it does. You can't find it. I've looked. I'll never stop looking." *Sandbox* means much of the activity involves living in a virtual world, rather than competing for points in a game. A dozen years after its death in 2011, *Star Wars Galaxies* has been resurrected, and Table 7 lists some YouTube videos documenting the current vitality of the community, with data collected on January 13, 2024.

The first of these videos was posted May 6, 2021, and its creator noted he missed Star Wars Day which has the pun blessing, "May the Fourth Be with You!" He offered this background: "Star Wars Galaxies went offline in 2011 but fan projects have brought the game back online! I'll be playing on the Legends server to see how this MMO Star Wars game holds up in the year 2021."[59] One of the written comments reports: "I've been playing SWG Legends for last few years. It's an awesome community, and just an all-around good time. Devs [developers] actively updating game, adding content. Free to play, but they accept donations to help keep things going. Thanks for checking out our little corner of the galaxy." Three of the videos have durations longer than one hour, and each explores at some depth one of the independent emulations: Restoration, SWGEmu, and Legends.

An online interview with a member of the Legends staff asked about the representative system for including players in decision-making, called a Senate, to which players were elected and that provided advice about current problems and future goals. The staff member expressed personal enthusiasm for partnership with players in virtual resurrection of SWG: "Both the Senate and the

---

[59] www.youtube.com/watch?v=S36C9ByeF9g.

Table 7 Recent YouTube videos about rogue servers

Title of Video	Duration	Days Online	Views per Day	Comments
I Played Star Wars Galaxies in 2021	18:36	983	332	1,028
Which Star Wars Galaxies Server to play In 2023?	6:03	748	52	313
Star Wars Galaxies in 2022!	20:58	712	215	471
Star Wars Galaxies Restoration!!! Zero to Hero!	1:25:45	468	11	30
How To Start Life In SWG / Star Wars Galaxies: SWGEmu	1:47:45	459	4	21
Star Wars Galaxies Legends – New Player Experience 2023	1:46:28	270	27	21
Star Wars Galaxies Online in 2023 is Unbelievable	13:39	263	2,477	1,480
Is Star Wars Galaxies Making a Comeback in 2023?	11:20	167	63	126
Star Wars Galaxies in 2023. It's Basically the Golden Age	24:21	164	966	384
Star Wars Galaxies and its Bright Future as an MMORPG	36:59	129	57	123
Which Star Wars Galaxies Server to play In 2024?	11:34	59	68	146

Senate committees are a complete asset to us. They're able to offer insight into a lot of the different aspects of the game we might otherwise not be able to see. All of our staff obviously love this game. We all play, and we're all into different areas whether it be space or ground combat, PvP, PvE, crafting, entertaining, doing endgame events, and we all have different areas that we like" (Brown 2023).

One of the comments on the most popular video, "Star Wars Galaxies Online in 2023 is Unbelievable," seemed to come from a different staff member: "I am one of the developers over at Legends. I have to say, fantastic video! The story of SWG near the end is a bit heartbreaking, but we strive to keep the dream alive. Thanks for the showcase and a fantastic video."[60] That comment received 161 written replies, including: "You are awesome, SWG is one of my all time favourite games. I have never felt sad over a game going 'offline' before like I did SWG. You guys bought that back and I hope you forever keep this game alive. I appreciate what you have done!"

The fact that multiple emulations are alive, even with some differences in style and with distinctive added content, indicates that SWG has become a complex social movement, if not a religious one. We could well imagine, however, that as they achieve independence from the commercial *Star Wars* franchise, players on the rogue servers might revive spiritual and even sacred aspects of Jediism, undertaking a religious *schism* from secularization, thus perhaps creating an ecology of Jedi *sects* rather than cults, culturally similar to each other but socially separated.

7 That Galaxy Far, Far Away

Hope for gaining vast rewards and avoiding deep costs is central to the *general compensator* theory of religion. While gaining subjective social status by "winning a game" is compensatory, the experience of hundreds of hours exploring vast virtual civilizations can serve as rewarding intellectual and ethical education for players, even as it earns real dollars for the game company (Castronova 2005). *Star Wars: The Old Republic* (SWTOR), built upon KotOR and currently represents nearly three dozen inhabited planets across the galaxy explored by Luke Skywalker (Searle 2011). It is set far back in time, around the year 3600 BBY, in which "BBY" is an abbreviation for "Before the Battle of Yavin," which was when Luke destroyed the Death Star in the first movie that dated from 1977 in a different calendar. So, this massively multiplayer online role-playing game, or virtual world, took place in ancient days, long before the Jedi had declined to a mere pair of hermit masters, Obi-Wan and Yoda. When creating an avatar, the player must select either

---

[60] www.youtube.com/watch?v=KSOP-gIJTcU.

the Republic or the Sith faction, and one of four classes in each faction, two of which have Force powers, while the other two do not but are more like the secular classes in *Star Wars Galaxies*. Each class has a different quest series that is extensive, thus offering fully eight main narratives at early experience levels, and many missions require deciding whether to earn ethics points on either the Light or Dark side of the Force. A social-scientific study based on interviews with 369 players found that many of them really do think philosophically about their avatar's ethical choices, and apply experience in the SWTOR virtual world to judgments about conflict in our real world (Geraci & Recine 2014).

A vast anthology of tales, SWTOR includes many that feature religious concepts. For example, a new Sith avatar in the Inquisitor class begins life on Korriban, a planet housing extensive underground ruins of the tomb of Tulak Hord, Master of the Gathering Darkness. This was the world where the Sith species had evolved, so it was holy in their history, especially after endless conflict caused it to be abandoned: "Retaking the holy planet of Korriban as a top priority, the Sith re-established the glorious Sith Academy and began training a new generation of Sith to inherit their dark legacy and seize their birthright as the true rulers of the galaxy."[61] After completing many training missions on Korriban and reaching experience level 10, the inquisitor travels to Dromund Kaas, where the Sith government has been established, both planets being within the same region of the galaxy, Seat of the Empire.

Several cults range across the surrounding wilderness and in the ruins of the Dark Temple. One is unusual but also primary in virtual history, the Order of Revan, with which the avatar can cooperate despite the fact it seeks to unite Dark and Light, Sith and Jedi.[62] Obviously, this links back to *Knights of the Old Republic*. At level 20, an inquisitor voyages to Nar Shaddaa, the Smuggler's Moon controlled by the Hutt Cartel, in a quest named The Prophet Arrives. Here is the introductory text from the online Jedipedia, in which the avatar's name would appear as <name>[63]:

> As tensions mount between the Empire and the Republic, <name>, apprentice to Darth Zash, leaves the confines of Imperial space in search of the lost artifacts of the legendary Dark Lord of the Sith, Tulak Hord. <name> heads to the decadent Hutt-controlled world of Nar Shaddaa to secure one of Tulak Hord's artifacts from the charismatic and egotistical Sith Lord Paladius, who has established a personal cult among the downtrodden of the glittering city-world. <name> approaches Paladius's former cultists with the plan of establishing a rival cult to force Paladius into handing over the artifact ...

---

[61] www.swtor.com/holonet/planets/korriban.

[62] starwars.fandom.com/wiki/Order_of_Revan; swtor.fandom.com/wiki/Revanite_Camp.

[63] swtor.jedipedia.net/en/qst/the-prophet-arrives.

After an initial battle, the Inquisitor avatar appeared in a pre-scripted "cut-scene" video and proclaimed, "Taking down oppressive cult leaders is a favorite hobby of mine." Soon, the avatar faces a choice, selecting which of two tactics to advance toward the new goal of gaining support from the masses of people oppressed by cults and gangs, either by killing gangsters or stealing from them medicines to cure a plague that was devastating "the poorest of Nar Shaddaa's poor." The first choice, killing, would strengthen the Dark Side of the avatar's character, while the second choice, curing, would strengthen the Light Side even of a Sith Inquisitor.

As Sith began on sacred Korriban, Jedi were given their early training on sacred Tython: "Mystical scholars gathered on the harsh and mysterious world of Tython millennia ago to begin the first studies of the Force, but controversy among the scholars' ranks created a cataclysm which nearly destroyed the planet. A small group of survivors fled to another star system, put their dark past behind them, and founded the Jedi Order."[64] Two very different planets were the starting points for mundane avatars who lacked connections with the Force, Ord Mantell for troopers and smugglers in the Republic, while the Empire's agents and bounty hunters began on Hutta which was dominated by giant slug gangsters called Hutts. During the first movie trilogy, their crime lord, Jaba the Hutt, was a major enemy, yet appeared in only 1.4 percent of the related AO3 stories.

In 2016, I did an initial survey, comparing avatar characteristics across servers using different languages. Of 2,395 English-speaking avatars, 69.1 percent belonged to the Jedi or Sith magical classes, rather similar to the 68.1 percent of 720 French avatars, and 64.8 percent of 1,696 German avatars (Bainbridge 2020b: 87). I was also able to survey 1,215 members of a remarkable community named Alea Iacta Est ("The die is cast") after the proclamation by Julius Caesar when his army crossed the Rubicon in the great game for power in Rome. AIE has multiple guilds across many online virtual worlds, and its members are unusually sophisticated game players, as suggested by the fact that only 54.2 percent played the four magical Jedi or Sith roles, and nearly equal fractions across the four secular classes. One interpretation of the difference between 69.1 percent and 54.2 is that individuals who enter SWTOR because they are *Star Wars* fans will emphasize the supernatural avatars, while the gamer subculture represented by AIE or SWG may not.

To measure the popularities of the factions and classes again after seven years of change, I expanded my avatar set from 7 to 12, equally in both Jedi Republic and Sith Empire, and had them join ordinary large player guilds. Belonging to a guild facilitated organizing teams to undertake group missions, using a search

---

[64] www.swtor.com/holonet/planets/tython.

Table 8 Class distribution of members of twelve large guilds

Faction	Class	Advanced	Republic	Empire
Republic	Jedi Knight	Guardian	15.4%	0.7%
		Sentinel	13.7%	0.6%
	Jedi Consular	Sage	11.9%	0.8%
		Shadow	13.7%	0.9%
	Trooper	Commando	7.2%	1.0%
		Vanguard	5.6%	1.0%
	Smuggler	Gunslinger	5.7%	1.4%
		Scoundrel	6.3%	1.3%
Empire	Sith Warrior	Marauder	1.6%	14.3%
		Juggernaut	2.6%	14.5%
	Sith Inquisitor	Assassin	2.4%	17.7%
		Sorcerer	2.8%	18.9%
	Imperial Agent	Operative	3.2%	8.0%
		Sniper	2.6%	6.2%
	Bounty Hunter	Powertech	1.8%	4.9%
		Mercenary	3.5%	8.0%
TOTAL			100.0%	100.0%
			4,071	3,873

system within SWTOR's computer interface that allowed me to copy out extensive data about the class, experience level, and current location of all member avatars. Table 8 reports results of a census done using this method in July 2023.

Originally, in SWTOR, a player created an avatar in a broadly defined class, such as Jedi Knight, then at level 10 of experience would select one of two advanced classes, in this case Guardian or Sentinel, with moderately different abilities. Early in 2022 a new expansion named Legacy of the Sith allowed an avatar to gain the skills of a different class. Although some old terminology continued, class was essentially redefined as *origin story*, keeping the class's traditional set of missions, while advanced class became *style*. This was easy for mundane classes, allowing an avatar with any of the four origin stories to begin with any of the eight styles. The supernatural Jedi and Sith avatars could take any of the four styles that belonged to their faction, then after completing the origin stories could earn a Force-related style from the other faction. To do this, a Jedi avatar needed to select many Dark Side actions, thus adopting Sith values, while a Sith would need to go far to the Light Side, adopting Jedi values.[65]

---

[65] swtorista.com/articles/choosing-a-class-in-swtor/.

Complexities like this not only added to the interesting episodes experienced by the player, and the profit of the game company as players paid their subscriptions longer, but also added philosophical elements in the tradition of *Knights of the Old Republic*.

The most obvious finding in Table 8 is that in 2023, as in 2016, the classes that use the Force are more popular than the ones that don't, the Sith plus Jedi classes totaling 66.2 percent of the avatars in the table. This difference is actually slightly lower than would have been the case before it was easy for non-Force avatars to have a class that actually belonged to the opposing faction. In the Empire, considering just the four traditional Imperial classes, 70.7 percent used the Force. The comparable Force faction for the Republic is 68.8 percent, essentially no difference. More generally, the table measures the result of SWTOR's strategy to retain active players, offering them not only eight novel-length story arcs, but many possible combinations of avatar characteristics.

A different way of contemplating that strategy is illustrated in Table 9, which lists the dozen avatars I created to do the research, in descending order of how many research hours I invested in each. The point of the following analysis is not to express personal pride, nor merely to illustrate the intensity and diversity of effort required from dedicated players, but to document the depth of the role-playing system. Players who were not constrained by research goals may often have similar sets of avatars, taking some to high levels of experience, while using others to explore the diversity of lower-level stories. The column labeled "AIs" counts how many companions each avatar earned, artificial characters one of which could go on a regular mission in support of the main avatar as in *Knights of the Old Republic*, while others could be assigned to invisible missions that earn small rewards, without graphic representation.

The first four avatars in the table were my initial research team, intentionally selected to cover both pairs of primary roles: factional alliance of Republic versus Empire, and class principle of Force versus secular. Especially when the research plan is to operate multiple avatars in a massively multiplayer online role-playing game, it is often valuable to adopt the *psychodrama* method of Jacob Moreno (1944, 1946), a pioneer in sociometry and the sociology of roles. He and his disciples primarily used it in group therapy sessions, where clients would take turns playing the role of a family member or other person relevant to the psychological problems the therapist sought to cure. Using the psychodrama method while role-playing during research allows one to compare multiple perspectives through the experiences of the avatars (Bainbridge 2023a). In *The Old Republic*, my four main avatars were based on four classic science fiction writers, each of whom greatly influenced the science fiction culture in which *Star Wars* arose (Bainbridge 2016: 114).

Table 9 A research team of diverse avatars

Faction	Species	Class	Advanced	Level	Hours	AIs	Final Location
Republic	Human	Jedi Knight	Sage	80	397	40	Dantooine
Republic	Human	Trooper	Vanguard	52	239	6	Republic Fleet
Empire	Zabrak	Sith Inquisitor	Sorcerer	70	211	13	Ossus
Empire	Cyborg	Imperial Agent	Sniper	51	182	6	Imperial Fleet
Republic	Twi'lek	Smuggler	Scoundrel	54	46	6	Alderaan
Republic	Mirialan	Jedi Consular	Guardian	51	32	6	Tatooine
Empire	Sith	Sith Warrior	Marauder	50	30	6	Corellia
Empire	Cyborg	Bounty Hunter	Mercenary	20	14	2	Hutta
Empire	Sith	Sith Inquisitor	Assassin	20	12	2	Nar Shaddaa
Republic	Togruta	Jedi Consular	Shadow	20	12	2	Coruscant
Empire	Zabrak	Smuggler	Gunslinger	20	10	1	Dromund Kass
Republic	Twi'lek	Jedi Knight	Sentinel	20	9	2	Tython

The primary avatar, who began the research on December 22, 2011 and reached the level 80 maximum after nearly four hundred hours, was based on the works concerning alien religion that significantly inspired *Star Wars*, by Burroughs (1917, 1918). The Trooper who would serve the Republic yet make many decisions for himself was based on Robert A. Heinlein (1959, 1961), whose novel *Starship Troopers* explored freedom within militarism, while *Stranger in a Strange Land* inspired the real new religious movement, The Church of All Worlds (Cusack 2010: 53–82). The Sith Inquisitor was based on Alfred Bester (1953), whose novel *The Demolished Man* explored human violence in a parareligious context through both psychoanalysis and telepathy. A member of the half-robot Cyborg species, the Imperial Agent, was based on Isaac Asimov (1954) who wrote extensively about robots, notably exploring the different limitations of human versus robot agents of violence in *The Caves of Steel*, giving robots far more autonomy than was enjoyed by R2-D2 or C-3PO. All four of the avatars reached the maximum experience level of 50 during the first phase of research, then in later phases Burroughs and Bester would explore new high-level planets that would bring the total to 32 worlds, as the experience cap rose to 80. The other eight avatars were created to explore a wider range of classes, stories, and planets.

Both Burroughs and Heinlein were Human, the most common species in the galaxy. Asimov was a Cyborg agent, a human being who had been augmented by computer hardware. Bester belonged to the apparently devilish Zabrak humanoid horned species, with a red skin given his Imperial faction, while Republican Zabraks have tan skins. We might assume that intelligent species that evolved on other planets might be physically very different from Humans, perhaps some shaped like spiders and others like bats. Yet movies tend to depict aliens like Humans, but with superficial differences in appearance, both to produce the movie more cheaply and to encourage the audience to empathize with the nicer extraterrestrials. Indeed, features on the head often distinguished two species that otherwise seemed very similar, allowing their movie actors to wear ordinary human clothing. For example, both Togruta and Twi'leks had fat tails on their heads, but shaped very differently. Each species had a distinctive history, notably the Sith Purebloods, a kind of character with currently special status within the Sith and Empire more generally. A special SWTOR wiki explains: "Descendants of the original Sith species, the red-skinned Sith purebloods inherit a legacy long intertwined with the dark side. The ancient Sith were warlike, competitive, and ambitious, and they performed arcane rituals to create powerful force artifacts."[66]

---

[66] swtor.fandom.com/wiki/Sith_Pureblood.

When I finish research of this kind, I always leave each avatar in a final location that is especially meaningful or offers a good starting location if I return to do more research. Each faction possessed a fleet of huge spaceships moored alongside a massive space station that served at its transportation and economic center. Two of the planets featured significantly in the original *Star Wars* movie: Tatooine and Alderaan. Tatooine, which we have linked to Barsoom and Arrakis, was where young Luke Skywalker was being raised by his uncle and aunt, not far from where Obi-Wan Kenobi was surviving as a hermit – an insignificant planet with a dry and empty environment. Alderaan is much more like Earth, with an environment naturally suited for life, and a large population in several cities and a coherent civilization. By the beginning of the first movie, Alderaan had become central to the Rebel Alliance seeking freedom from the Empire. It is the home planet of Princess Leia Organa.

What was the fate of Alderaan? Soon after her capture by Darth Vader, Princess Leia Organa was forced to witness Alderaan's total destruction by the Death Star, causing millions of deaths. An article in *Bulletin of the Atomic Scientists* reveals: "The Death Star ... serves as a stand-in for the nuclear weapons arsenal with all the accompanying nuclear imagery, deterrence theory, and dangers shown to the audience" (Westmyer 2017). Indeed, what is the meaning of "scientific progress" in our own world where weapons that could destroy everything have been developed, manufactured in great numbers, and held by hostile nations that seem nearly ready to descend into war? A religious person might make the rather convincing argument that all humanity must unite in a single church worshiping one God who preserves peace by demanding abandonment of the evil elements, Uranium and Plutonium, and by filling our souls with love for each other. Yet our planet is secularizing at a desperate hour, even as conflicts both religious and secular seem to be increasing beyond control. A favorite alternative solution of science fiction fans, inhabiting many planets so that destruction will always be limited to just one, is physically impossible (Cavelos 1999). The recent commercial history of *Star Wars* movies and streaming TV series, which has diminished the significance of the Jedi and the Force, raises doubts about the feasibility of religious revival, even as a parareligion.

8 The Secular Trend

In 2012, the Walt Disney Company purchased the *Star Wars* franchise and soon produced the sequel trilogy of movies plus two other movies and dozens of episodes of streaming series. This had the ironic effect of promoting sales at the cost of spirituality, that may have discouraged building a real world religion upon it as some Jedi wished to do. Vast numbers of fans rated the movies at the Internet Movie Database, giving the first trilogy an average rating of 8.5 on a 1–10 scale, November 24, 2023, compared with 6.9 for the prequel trilogy. The average for Disney's sequel trilogy was a slightly more favorable 7.0, but its three movies differed: *The Force Awakens* (7.8), *The Last Jedi* (6.9), and *The Rise of Skywalker* (6.4).[67]

A special session of the 2016 meetings of the American Academy of Religion considered the religious significance of *Star Wars* in the context of *The Force Awakens*, resulting in a book with the title *The Myth Awakens* by eleven authors (Derry & Lyden 2018). It well documents many of the ways that members of the general public may read their own meanings into the mythos, but mentions serious Jediism only rarely. For example, in a discussion of Disney taking ownership of the copyrights, MacKendrick (2018: 151) notes that "Jediism may be viewed best not as a subculture of *Star Wars* fandom but as a niche strategy for particular kinds of political or social protest." With more concern for Jediism and critical of how Disney seemed to be demoting fans to mere customers, Hussain (2018: 143) proclaimed: "The fundamental schism created by de-canonization and revision in the *Star Wars* universe should be conceived as a crisis of collective memory or as a break in the chain of a tradition." The positive general tone of *The Myth Awakens* is more like hope that *The Force Awakens* is a revival or even a resurrection, that would give new life to this community-based mythos.

Two of the nine chapters focused on the very difficult issue of racism, specifically the greater diversity of actors in *The Force Awakens* than in the earlier films, that drew some public criticism. Notably an actor of Nigerian descent played the role of Finn who had been a stormtrooper of the First Order that seeks to restore the Empire, but defected for ethical reasons to the Resistance (Call 2018; Hodge & Boston 2018). If *Star Wars* were strict science fiction, we might have expected that people from different planets would be biologically rather different from each other, as in James Cameron's 2009 film, *Avatar*, where the people of the planet Pandora are blue in color. In *The Myth Awakens*, Call (2018: 102) praises two games we have emphasized here, *Knights of the Old Republic* and SWTOR, because "players can create diverse hero characters by defining through the interface the racial and physical dynam-ics of the player avatar."

The 2015–2019 trilogy includes standard features such as lightsaber duels, battles between fleets of spaceships, and dynamic social relations among central characters, but it does nothing to promote a more sophisticated sense that

---

[67] www.imdb.com/star-wars/.

Jediism could become a viable religion, even though ethical issues were included in the narratives. Already in *The Force Awakens*, an elderly Luke Skywalker prepares for the end of the Jedi, and in *The Last Jedi,* he sacrifices his life. *The Rise of Skywalker* ends not with his rebirth, but the death of his sister, Princess Leia, already well after the death of the actress who played her role. The Skywalker who rises is the only remaining Jedi, a young woman named Rey who chose to adopt that family name. On April 7, 2023, the franchise announced that three more films are planned, including one to be "set after the events of *Star Wars: Rise of Skywalker*, and feature Daisy Ridley back as Rey as she builds a new Jedi Order."[68] A possibility remains, then, that Disney might add cultural elements supportive of Jediism, but at present its religious contribution is simply promoting the high popularity of its *Star Wars* products and thus of the mythos more generally.

In a huge convention of fans meeting before release of the second those films, the actor who played Luke, Mark Hamill, expressed some dismay about where the story was going: "How did the most optimistic hopeful character in the galaxy turn into this hermit who says it's time for the Jedi to end? I read that, and I said 'What?' I mean, that's not what a Jedi does. I mean, a Jedi is optimistic. A Jedi has tenacity. He never gives up." Those words were transcribed from a YouTube video posted March 30, 2018 that by January 3, 2024 had gathered 7,220,852 views and a remarkable 25,612 comments, including one that earned 207 replies: "There needs to be a documentary about what went wrong with Star Wars. Directed, written and narrated by Mark Hamill."[69] Another video posted February 6, 2022, broadens the critique hinted by its title: "The Star Wars Sequels: Disney's Anti-Trilogy." It quickly earned 3,965,347 views and 24,151 comments, one of which earned 500 replies: "The sequels did one thing right. They made the majority of Star Wars fans greatly appreciate the prequels!"[70]

The 2016 non-trilogy movie, *Rogue One*, provided a part of the original story that had been missing, namely the events that gave Princess Leia the plans to the Death Star. But it was rather gloomy because it ended with the deaths of many new heroic characters it had introduced. Remarkably, actor Peter Cushing reprised the important enemy role of Grand Moff Tarkin, which he had played in the original *Star Wars*, despite having died in 1994. A combination of a substitute actor and computer graphics were able to achieve a realistic "digital resurrection" (Tapley & Debruge 2016). In the movie itself, one of the heroes fated to die expressed some faith in the Force while lacking full supernatural

---

[68] www.starwars.com/news/swce-2023-new-star-wars-films.
[69] www.youtube.com/watch?v=WKlo-plLJZI.
[70] www.youtube.com/watch?v=XtArKawnWNI.

powers and not being a Jedi: "The Force is with me. And I am with the Force. And I fear nothing. For all is as the Force wills it." Those are the key words of Chirrut Îmwe, a blind member of a monastic order named Guardians of the Whills, who can magically move like a highly skilled Samurai under the fatalistic guidance of the Force. As Wookieepedia states, "While the Force can grant users powerful abilities, it also directs their actions. And it has a will of its own, which both scholars and mystics have spent millennia seeking to understand."[71] If the Force "has a will of its own," is it a conscious god? Or is that just a metaphor?

The second non-trilogy film, *Solo*, which was released in 2018, offered more of the original 1977 story and tells how Han Solo teamed up with Chewbacca and obtained the Millenium Falcon spaceship. But it includes essentially nothing about the Jedi. There is a very brief video communication near the end with the former Sith lord who had been named Darth Maul, but was now simply Maul and a gang leader who had incidentally kept his lightsaber. Wikipedia reports: "Star Wars creator George Lucas had intended for the resurrected Maul to serve as the main antagonist of the sequel film trilogy, but these plans were abandoned when Disney acquired Lucasfilm in 2012."[72]

Near the end of my 2023 phase of research on real-world Jedi communities, I attended an online Zoom meeting of representatives of several religious Jediist groups who discussed how Jedi could actually contribute to the welfare of humanity. Some apparently had regular jobs in social work broadly defined, but also advocated volunteer work in traditional organizations, and felt comfortable combining Jediism with their own heritages in Christianity, Judaism, and Buddhism. While the overwhelming emphasis in the recent movies and streaming series is on violence, the discussion prioritized charity, providing help to fellow human beings in hopes of liberating them from their suffering. While expressing their benevolent personal values, these Jedis reflected the challenge their wider community had faced in seeking formal status as a religion. Participants in each of the social media differ in terms of how much their veneration of the Force qualifies as religion, versus parareligion or pure fiction. Possibly in a diverse spiritual community, there may be a symbiotic relationship between religion and parareligion, each strengthening the other. So the future of Jediism may depend not only upon the future of the commercial franchise, but even more significantly on which human spiritual, cognitive and psychological needs are poorly satisfied if secularization of the surrounding civilization continues.

---

[71] www.starwars.com/databank/the-force.   [72] en.wikipedia.org/wiki/Darth_Maul.

References

Ammerman, N. T. (2013). Spiritual but not religious? Beyond binary choices in the study of religion. *Journal for the Scientific Study of Religion*, 52(2): 258–78.

Asimov, I. (1954). *The Caves of Steel*. New York: Doubleday.

Bainbridge, W. S. (1978). *Satan's Power: A Deviant Psychotherapy Cult*. Berkeley, CA: University of California Press.

Bainbridge, W. S. (1986). *Dimensions of Science Fiction*. Cambridge, MA: Harvard University Press.

Bainbridge, W. S. (1997). *The Sociology of Religious Movements*. New York: Routledge.

Bainbridge, W. S. (2002). A prophet's reward: Dynamics of religious exchange. In T. G. Jelen, ed., *Sacred Markets, Sacred Canopies*. Lanham, MD: Rowman and Littlefield, pp. 63–89.

Bainbridge, W. S. (2003). Privacy and property on the net: Research questions. *Science*, 302: 1686–87.

Bainbridge, W. S. (2004). After the new age. *Journal for the Scientific Study of Religion*, 43(3): 381–94.

Bainbridge, W. S. (2010). *Online Multiplayer Games*. San Rafael, CA: Morgan and Claypool.

Bainbridge, W. S. (2013). *eGods: Faith versus Fantasy in Computer Gaming*. New York: Oxford University Press.

Bainbridge, W. S. (2015). The paganization process. *Interdisciplinary Journal of Research on Religion*, vol. 11, article no. 14. www.religjournal.com/articles/article_view.php?id=105.

Bainbridge, W. S. (2016). *Star Worlds: Freedom versus Control in Online Gameworlds*. Ann Arbor, MI: University of Michigan Press.

Bainbridge, W. S. (2017). *Dynamic Secularization: Information Technology and Tension between Religion and Science*. London: Springer.

Bainbridge, W. S. (2020a). Age of Conan. *World Religions and Spirituality*, wrldrels.org/2020/01/21/conan/.

Bainbridge, W. S. (2020b). *The Social Structure of Online Communities*. Cambridge: Cambridge University Press.

Bainbridge, W. S. (2023a). Dimensions of online role-playing: Anchored in the Tolkien mythos. *Social Science Computer Review*, 41(4): 1473–92.

Bainbridge, W. S. (2023b). The global revival of legendism: Korean online games. *International Journal for the Study of New Religions*, 12(1): 55–76.

Bainbridge, W. S. (2023c). The virtual rebirth of Paganism. *Journal of Religion, Film, and Media*, 9(1): 45–68.

Bainbridge, W. S., & Stark, R. (1979). Cult formation: Three compatible models. *Sociological Analysis*, 40(4): 283–95.

Bainbridge, W. S., & Stark, R. (1980). Client and audience cults in America. *Sociological Analysis*, 41: 199–214.

Baker, V. J. (1987). Pitching a tent in the native village: Malinowski and participant observation. *Bijdragen tot de Taal-, Land- en Volkenkunde*, 143(1): 14–24.

Barker, E. (2014). The not-so-new religious movements: Changes in "the cult scene" over the past forty years. *Temenos*, 50(2): 235–56.

Becker, H. S., & Geer, B. (1957). Participant observation and interviewing: A comparison. *Human Organization*, 16(3): 28–32.

Bester, A. (1953). *The Demolished Man*. Chicago, IL: Shasta.

Borowik, C. (2023). *From Radical Jesus People to Virtual Religion: The Family International*. Cambridge: Cambridge University Press.

Bortolin, M. (2015). *The Dharma of Star Wars*. Somerville, MA: Wisdom.

Britt, R. (2023). Star Wars just copied another brilliant sci-fi concept from Dune. *Inverse*, www.inverse.com/entertainment/star-wars-dune-ahsoka-nightsisters-bene-gesserit.

Brown, J. (2023). Star Wars Galaxies: Legends interview. *Game Rant*, Novembe 20, gamerant.com/star-wars-galaxies-legends-interview/.

Brown, T. (2023). Commentary: "Ahsoka" proves that "Star Wars" has long been a galaxy where women can be heroes. *Los Angeles Times*, August 23, www.latimes.com/entertainment-arts/tv/story/2023–08–23/ahsoka-star-wars-rebels-sabine-wren-hera-syndulla.

Burroughs, E. R. (1917). *A Princess of Mars*. Chicago, IL: A. C. McClurg.

Burroughs, E. R. (1918). *Gods of Mars*. Chicago, IL: A. C. McClurg.

Call, J. (2018). Do, or do not; there is no try: Race, rhetoric, and diversity in the *Star Wars* universe. In K. Derry, and J. C. Lyden, eds., *The Myth Awakens*. Eugene, OR: Cascade, pp. 92–105.

Callaway, K. (2018). I've heard this somewhere before: The myth-making implications of Han and Leia's theme. In K. Derry, and J. C. Lyden, eds., *The Myth Awakens*. Eugene, OR: Cascade, pp. 61–73.

Campbell, J. (2005). *The Hero with a Thousand Faces*. Princeton: Princeton University Press.

Campbell, H. A. (2013). Community. In H. Campbell, ed., *Digital Religion*. London: Routledge, pp. 57–71.

Castronova, E. (2005). *Synthetic Worlds: The Business and Culture of Online Games*. Chicago, IL: University of Chicago Press.

Cavelos, J. (1999). *The Science of Star Wars*. New York: St. Martin's Press.

Chen, C. (2022). *Work Pray Code: When Work Becomes Religion in Silicon Valley*. Princeton: Princeton University Press.

Chidester, D. (2003). Fake religion: Ordeals of authenticity in the study of religion. *Journal for the Study of Religion*, 16(2): 71–97.

Christopher, A. J. (2006). Questions of identity in the millennium round of commonwealth censuses. *Population Studies*, 60(3), 343–52.

Coleridge, S. T. (1817). *Biographia Literaria*. New York: Kirk and Merein.

Cormier, R. (1990). The closed society and its friends: Plato's "Republic" and Lucas's "THX-1138." *Literature/Film Quarterly*, 18(3): 193–97.

Crosby, J. (2022). The Complete list of Star Wars Galaxies rogue servers. *MMO Folklorist*, mmofolklorist.com/2022/07/25/the-complete-list-of-star-wars-galaxies-rogue-servers-2022/.

Cusack, C. M. (2010). *Invented Religions: Imagination, Fiction and Faith*. Farnham: Ashgate.

Davidsen, M. A. (2013). Fiction-based religion: Conceptualising a new category against history-based religion and fandom. *Culture and Religion*, 14(4): 378–95.

Davidsen, M. A. (2016). The religious affordances of fiction: A semiotic approach. *Religion*, 46(4): 521–49.

Davidsen, M. A. (2017). The Jedi community: History and folklore of a fiction-based religion. *New Directions in Folklore*, 15(1–2): 7–49.

Davidsen, M. (2018). Jedi community. *World Religions and Spirituality Project*, wrldrels.org/2018/02/21/jedi-community/.

De Vaucouleurs, G. (1950). *The Planet Mars*. London: Faber and Faber.

Decker, K. S., & Eberl, J. T., eds. (2005). *Star Wars and Philosophy: More Powerful than You Can Possibly Imagine*. Chicago, IL: Carus.

Demerath, N. J. (2000). The varieties of sacred experience: Finding the sacred in a secular grove. *Journal for the Scientific Study of Religion*, 39(1): 1–11.

Derry, K., & Lyden, J. C., eds. (2018). *The Myth Awakens*. Eugene, OR: Cascade.

Derschowitz, J. (2017). Star Wars: The Last Jedi is dedicated to Carrie Fisher. *Entertainment Weekly*, ew.com/movies/2017/12/12/star-wars-the-last-jedi-carrie-fisher-tribute/.

DiMaggio, P. J., & Anheier, H. K. (1990). The sociology of nonprofit organizations. *Annual Review of Sociology*, 16: 137–59.

Dym, B., & Fiesler, C. (2020). Ethical and privacy considerations for research using online fandom data. *Transformative Works and Cultures*, 33. journal.transformativeworks.org/index.php/twc/article/view/1733/2445.

Elm, M. S. (2009). How do various notions of privacy influence decisions in qualitative internet research? In A. N. Markham, and N. K. Baym, eds., *Internet Inquiry: Conversations about Method*. Los Angeles, CA: Sage, pp. 69–98.

Eynon, R., Fry, J., & Schroeder, R. (2008). The ethics of internet research. In N. Fielding, R. M. Lee, and G. Blank, eds., *The Sage Handbook of Online Research Methods*. Thousand Oaks, CA: Sage, pp. 23–41.

Farley, H. (2017). Virtual knights and synthetic worlds. In C. M. Cusack, and P. Kosnáč, eds., *Fiction, Invention, and Hyper-reality: From Popular Culture to Religion*. Farnham: Ashgate, pp. 134–47.

Festinger, L., Riecken, H. W., & Schachter, S. (1956). *When Prophecy Fails*. Minneapolis, MN: University of Minnesota Press.

Feuerverger, A., He, Y., & Khatri, S. (2012). Statistical significance of the Netflix challenge. *Statistical Science*, 27(2): 202–31.

Geraci, R. M., & Recine, N. (2014). Enlightening the galaxy: How players perceive political philosophy in Star Wars: The Old Republic. *Games & Culture*, 9(4): 255–76.

Gray, C. (2017). *Star Wars: Leia, Princess of Alderaan*. Los Angeles, CA: Disney.

Grieve, G. P. (2013). Religion. In H. Campbell, ed., *Digital Religion*. London: Routledge, pp. 104–18.

Grinker, R. R. (2000). *In the Arms of Africa*. New York: St. Martin's.

Hammer, O., & Swartz-Hammer, K. (2024). *New Religious Movements and Comparative Religion*. Cambridge: Cambridge University Press.

Heinlein, R. A. (1959). *Starship Troopers*. New York: G. P. Putnam's Sons.

Heinlein, R. A. (1961). *Stranger in a Strange Land*. New York: G. P. Putnam's Sons.

Heldman, M. E. (1992). Architectural symbolism, sacred and the Ethiopian church. *Journal of Religion in Africa*, 22(3): 222–41.

Herbert, F. (1965). *Dune*. Boston, MA: Chilton.

Herrigel, E. (1953). *Zen in the Art of Archery*. New York: Pantheon.

Hoberman, B. (1983). The Ethiopian legend of the Ark. *The Biblical Archaeologist*, 46(2): 113–14.

Hobson, J. (2017). Euhemerism and the veiling of history in early Scandinavian literature. *The Journal of English and German Philology*, 116(1): 24–44.

Hodge, D. A., & Boston, J. (2018). The racism awakens. In K. Derry, and J. C. Lyden, eds., *The Myth Awakens*. Eugene, OR: Cascade, pp. 74–91.

Holmes, R. (2017). Charity Commission decision: The Temple of the Jedi Order. Farrer, www.farrer.co.uk/news-and-insights/charity-commission-deci sion-the-temple-of-the-jedi-order/.

Hori, V. S. (2016). D. T. Suzuki and the invention of tradition. *The Eastern Buddhist*, 47(2): 41–81.

Horowitz, N. H. (1986). Mars: Myth and reality. *Engineering & Science*, 49(4): 4–37.

Hussain, S. A. (2018). Memory, history and forgetting in *Star Wars* fandom. In K. Derry, and J. C. Lyden, eds., *The Myth Awakens*. Eugene, OR: Cascade, pp. 133–46.

Jacobsson, K., & Lindblom, J. (2016). *Animal Rights Activism*. Amsterdam: Amsterdam University Press.

Johns, M. D. (2013). Ethical issues in the study of religion and new media. In H. Campbell, ed., *Digital Religion*. London: Routledge, pp. 238–50.

Jones, D. M. (2017). *Become the Force*. London: Watkins.

Kasselstrand, I., Zuckerman, P., & Cragun, R. T. (2023). *Beyond Doubt: The Secularization of Society*. New York: New York University Press.

Kinnard, R., Crnkovich, T., & Vitrone, R. J. (2005). *The Flash Gordon Serials, 1936–1940*. Jefferson, MO: McFarland.

Lacy, N. J. (2005). Medieval McGuffins: The Arthurian model. *Arthuriana*, 15(4): 53–64.

Lethbridge, T. (2021). Everything Star Wars took from Dune. *Screen Rant*, screenrant.com/star-wars-dune-story-concepts-ideas-lucas-copy/.

Littlefair, S. (2015). Was Yoda based on this Buddhist master? *Lion's Roar*, www.lionsroar.com/was-yoda-based-on-this-buddhist-master/.

Lofland, J., & Stark, R. (1965). Becoming a world-saver. *American Sociological Review*, 30(6): 862–75.

Lowell, P. (1906). *Mars and Its Canals*. New York: Macmillan.

Lowell, P. (1908). *Mars as the Abode of Life*. New York: Macmillan.

Lyden, J. C. (2012). Whose film is it, anyway? Canonicity and authority in "Star Wars" fandom. *Journal of the American Academy of Religion*, 80(3): 775–86.

MacKendrick, K. (2018). The ion *canon* will fire several shots to make sure any enemy ships will fly out of your flight path. In K. Derry, and J. C. Lyden, eds., *The Myth Awakens*. Eugene, OR: Cascade, pp. 147–62.

McCubbin, C. (2005). *Star Wars Galaxies: The Complete Guide*. Roseville, CA: Prima Games.

McCubbin, C., Ladyman, D., & Frase, T., eds. (2005). *Star Wars Galaxies: The Total Experience*. Roseville, CA: Prima Games.

McDowell, J. C. (2007). *The Gospel According to Star Wars: Faith, Hope and the Force*. Louisville, KY: John Knox Press.

Merton, R. K. (1938). Social structure and anomie. *American Sociological Review*, 3(5): 672–82.

Miller, C. (2016). Spiritual but not religious: Rethinking the legal definition of religion. *Virginia Law Review*, 102(3): 833–94.

Monges, M. M. (2002). The Queen of Sheba and Solomon: Exploring the Shebanization of knowledge. *Journal of Black Studies*, 33(2): 235–46.

Moreno, J. L. (1944). Psychodrama and therapeutic motion pictures. *Sociometry*, 7, 230–44.

Moreno, J. L. (1946). Psychodrama and group therapy. *Sociometry*, 9, 249–53.

Moyers, B., & Lucas, G. (1999). Of myth and men. *Time*, content.time.com/time/magazine/article/0,9171,23298-2,00.html.

Oh, S., & Sarkisian, N. (2012). Spiritual individualism or engaged spirituality? Social implications of holistic spirituality among mind-body-spirit practitioners. *Sociology of Religion*, 73(3): 299–322.

Olivetti, J. (2015). Star Wars Galaxies' NGE. *Massively Overpowered*, August 22, massivelyop.com/2015/08/22/the-game-archaeologist-star-wars-galaxies-nge/.

Possamai, A. (2011). Gramsci, Jediism, the standardization of popular religion and the state. In J. Barbalet, A. Possamai, and B. S. Turner, eds., *Religion and the State*. London: Anthem Press, pp. 245–62.

Prohl, I. (2014). California "Zen": Buddhist spirituality made in America. *Amerikastudien / American Studies*, 59(2): 193–206.

Radde-Antweiler, K. (2013). Authenticity. In H. Campbell, ed., *Digital Religion*. London: Routledge, pp. 88–103.

Reps, P. (1957). *Zen Flesh, Zen Bones*. Rutland, VT: C. E. Tuttle.

Richardson, J. T., Best, J. & Bromley, D. (1991). *The Satanism Scare*. New York: Aldine de Gruyter.

Rinzer, J. W. (2007). *The Making of Star Wars*. New York: Ballantine.

Robinson, W. R. (2005). The far east of Star Wars. In K. S. Decker, and J. T. Eberl, eds., *Star Wars and Philosophy*. Chicago, IL: Open Court, pp. 29–38.

Ross, J. C. (2021). Buddhism in Star Wars. *The Human Front*, www.thehumanfront.com/buddhism-in-star-wars/.

Royce, B. (2023). My 20 years of Star Wars Galaxies. *Massively Overpowered*, massivelyop.com/2023/06/26/working-as-intended-my-20-years-of-star-wars-galaxies/.

Searle, M. (2011). *Star Wars the Old Republic Explorer's Guide*. Roseville, CA: Prima Games.

Sharf, R. H. (1993). The Zen of Japanese nationalism. *History of Religions*, 33(1): 1–43.

Shoji, Y. (2001). The myth of Zen in the art of archery. *Japanese Journal of Religious Studies*, 28: 1–25.

Smelser, N. J. (1962). *Theory of Collective Behavior*. New York: Free Press.

Snodgrass, J. G. (2023). *The Avatar Faculty: Ecstatic Transformations in Religion and Video Games*. Berkeley, CA: University of California Press.

Stark, R., & Bainbridge, W. S. (1985). *The Future of Religion*. Berkeley, CA: University of California Press.

Stark, R., & Bainbridge, W. S. (1987). *A Theory of Religion*. New York: Peter Lang.

Suzuki, D. T. (1956). *Zen Buddhism*. Garden City, NY: Doubleday.

Suzuki, D. T., Fromm, E., & De Martino, R. (1960). *Zen Buddhism and Psychoanalysis*. New York: Harper.

Tapley, K., & Debruge, P. (2016). "Rogue One": What Peter Cushing's digital resurrection means for the industry. Variety, variety.com/2016/film/news/rogue-one-peter-cushing-digital-resurrection-cgi-1201943759/.

Thorvaldsen, G. (2014). Religion in the census. *Social Science History*, 38(1–2): 203–20.

Tolkien, J. R. R. (2008). *Tolkien on Fairy-stories*. London: Harper Collins.

Trowbridge, J. T. (1908). Early investigations in Spiritualism, *The North American Review*, 188(635): 526–38.

Van Gennep, A. (1909). *The Rites of Passage*. London: Routledge & Paul.

Wagner, Richard. (1895). The art-work of the future. In *Richard Wagner's Prose Works*. Ed. William Ashton Ellis, pp. 69–213. London: K. Paul, Trench.

Wagner, Rachel (2012). *Godwired: Religion, Ritual and Virtual Reality*. London: Routledge.

Wallace, D. (2012). *The Jedi Path*. San Francisco, CA: Chronicle Books.

Wallace, D. (2015). *Book of Sith*. Belleview, FL: Becker and Mayer.

Watts, A. (1957). *The Way of Zen*. New York: Pantheon.

Watts, A. (1961). *Psychotherapy East and West*. New York: Pantheon.

Westmyer, T. (2017). Death star: Ultimate weapon of mass destruction. *Bulletin of the Atomic Scientists*, thebulletin.org/2017/01/death-star-ultimate-weapon-of-mass-destruction/.

Wetmore, K. J. (2000). The Tao of "Star Wars," or, cultural appropriation in a galaxy far, far away. *Studies in Popular Culture*, 23(1): 91–106.

Whitney-Robinson, V., & Blackman, H. (2004). *Star Wars Galaxies: The Ruins of Dantooine*. New York: Ballantine.

Williams, S. (2008). *Star Wars: The Force Unleashed*. New York: Ballantine.

Young, B. (2019). "Star Wars" owes a great debt to Akira Kurosawa's "The Hidden Fortress." *SlashFilm*, www.slashfilm.com/567916/star-wars-and-the-hidden-fortress/.

Cambridge Elements ☰

New Religious Movements

Founding Editor

†James R. Lewis

Wuhan University

The late James R. Lewis was a Professor of Philosophy at Wuhan University, China. He was the author or co-author of 128 articles and reference book entries, and editor or co-editor of 50 books. He was also the general editor for the *Alternative Spirituality and Religion Review* and served as the associate editor for the *Journal of Religion and Violence*. His prolific publications include *The Cambridge Companion to Religion and Terrorism* (Cambridge University Press 2017) and *Falun Gong: Spiritual Warfare and Martyrdom* (Cambridge University Press 2018).

Series Editor

Rebecca Moore

San Diego State University

Rebecca Moore is Emerita Professor of Religious Studies at San Diego State University. She has written and edited numerous books and articles on Peoples Temple and the Jonestown tragedy. Publications include *Beyond Brainwashing: Perspectives on Cultic Violence* (Cambridge University Press 2018) and *Peoples Temple and Jonestown in the Twenty-First Century* (Cambridge University Press 2022). She is reviews editor for *Nova Religio*, the quarterly journal on new and emergent religions published by the University of Pennsylvania Press.

About the Series

Elements in New Religious Movements go beyond cult stereotypes and popular prejudices to present new religions and their adherents in a scholarly and engaging manner. Case studies of individual groups, such as Transcendental Meditation and Scientology, provide in-depth consideration of some of the most well known, and controversial, groups. Thematic examinations of women, children, science, technology, and other topics focus on specific issues unique to these groups. Historical analyses locate new religions in specific religious, social, political, and cultural contexts. These examinations demonstrate why some groups exist in tension with the wider society and why others live peaceably in the mainstream. The series highlights the differences, as well as the similarities, within this great variety of religious expressions. To discuss contributing to this series please contact Professor Moore.

Cambridge Elements ⁼

New Religious Movements

Printed in the United States
by Baker & Taylor Publisher Services